Marja
AF406895
The Art of Living and Learning
A Guide to Unlocking Your Inner
Strenght and Potential

Marjana Robavs

THE ART OF LIVING AND LEARNING

A Guide to Unlocking Your Inner Strength and Potential

Illustrations
Radovan Jenko

CONTENT

The moment I published my book was a turning point in my life. When I wrote it in 2020, I didn't realize the impact it would have on my readers and me. It all happened so quickly that I couldn't comprehend the significance of what I had accomplished—not just for others but for myself. Reading the feedback from my readers was genuinely heartwarming, and I realized that I had created something wonderful and valuable.  ⁝ Meeting people who read my book enriched my life in many ways. One encounter, in particular, was exceptional. I reunited with someone I had known for over thirty years, and our connection was reignited through my book. But that's a story for another chapter or even another book. ⁝ I decided to translate my book's second, updated edition into English and share it with the world. And now, it's in your hands. ⁝ Everything happens at the right time and in the proper sequence. There are no coincidences, and on our life's journey, we always meet people who are vibrationally aligned with us and show us what's happening within us. ⁝ The universe always knows when two people are ready to meet. It knows a perfect time. It always sends us the right person at the right time. We meet when we're prepared for each other. ⁝ It's no coincidence that you're reading my book right now. Enjoy your journey. ⁝⁝ *Marjana*

This book is about bitter and sweet experiences, frustrating and revealing, and even those you've kept hidden. It talks about reality, misconceptions, expectations, dreams, desires, and mistakes. In short, it's about life. The stories in this book are enriched with insights, bitter and sweet moments. Still, above all, they are about the desire and determination to tackle things you may not have dealt with before and do it in your own style—uncompromisingly and decisively. ⋮ You've got what it takes. You have the recipe for transferring your experiences, not selling them. You would have sold them if it weren't for you being in this book. But there's so much of you in it (in fact, all of you) that it's not about selling but transferring. Essentially, you're

passing on your years of experience to the reader or, preferably, to my daughters. And for that, I am infinitely grateful. You have given them the most beautiful, best, and most unforgettable gift. ⋮ And that's that. ⋮ »Coming back« crossed my mind many times while reading this book. Of course, I reviewed the index to see if you titled any chapter as such (Coming back). You didn't, and I was overjoyed. ⋮ Yes, exactly. That's the essence of this book. Coming back. You come back to it. You come back to the stories you've already read. Why? Because it feels good, because you feel like you didn't fully understand, comprehend, accept, or admit everything the first time around ... because you feel like you need to reread a chapter because something happened to you that is connected to a specific chapter in the book . . . because you need confirmation of your thoughts, your attitude toward the world, people, your environment, colleagues, neighbors ... ⁝ In short, you return to your book. And that means it's a good book. Because you want to read it constantly and draw from it. ⁝ This act of returning makes the book and the author great. ⁝⁝ *Your (proud) brother*

Writing this book was inspired by a letter I received from Svitlana Buko. At the time, she was just an acquaintance, but now she is a dear friend.

Marjana,

I am smiling and remembering our terrific lunch talk.

I agree with you on all of the aspects of life design and

it's a big important philosophy concept of life!

You have a clear vision and so many great examples

of life design - it's true that many people

would benefit from YOUR book :)

I completely agree with all the other people

who told you that your knowledge and MINDSET

are worth a book :)

Your stories about life design projects

are just mind-blowing!

Hugs, Svitlana

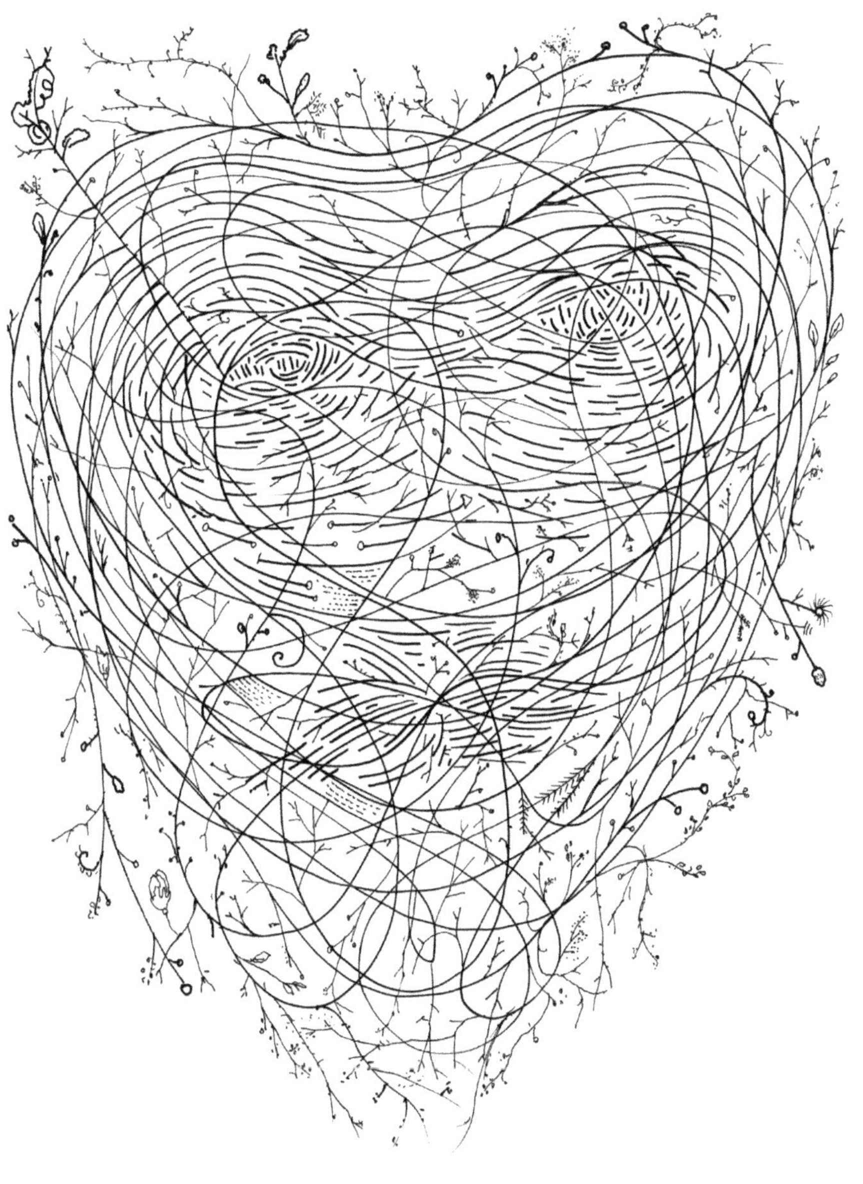

Welcome to the book that's been a part of my life journey, and now I get to share it with you. I wrote this for you because I love you and believe that the wisdom and experience I've gained will benefit you somehow. ⋮ I understand that life isn't always easy, and I wouldn't want to protect you from failure. In fact, it's the exact opposite. The challenges and obstacles you'll face will shape you into the person you're meant to be. And that's why this book is here—to help you navigate life's ups and downs and find your own path. ⋮ I want you to know that there's no rushing through life. You must go through the right experiences and reach maturity before truly discovering yourself. And that's okay. Embrace where you're at and make the most of every moment. ⋮ You're in control of your own life. Don't let others dictate how you should live. Do what makes you happy, and don't waste time regretting or feeling wrong about past experiences. Everything happens for a reason, leading you to where you're meant to be. ⋮ So go ahead, take the reins, and make the most of this journey called life. I trust you and know you have what it takes to unleash your full potential. ⋮ Yours truly, ⋮ Marjana ⦂⦂

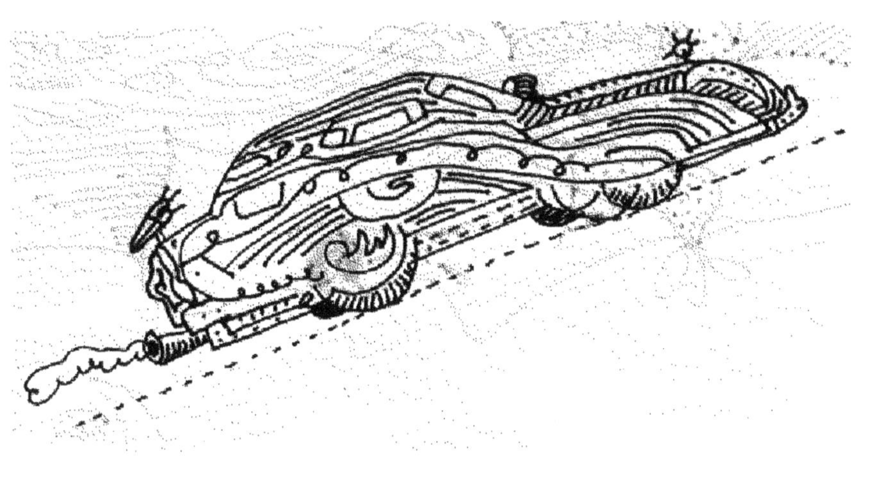

My driving instructor was a wise man. At the time, he seemed old but was younger than me. He started our first lesson with these words: »Marjana, in the beginning, the car drives you, and it doesn't feel good. Only when you've driven many kilometers, faced difficult and unpredictable situations, and gained enough experience can you start driving it. That's when you begin to enjoy the ride.« I was eighteen at the time and didn't understand everything he meant. ⁝ Life is the same way. Life drives us when we're young and inexperienced, not the other way around. In fact, our lives are like our cars. The first car is usually inherited from our parents and more

to their taste than ours. But when we recover and know what we want, we choose one that suits us best at that time in terms of size, shape, power, and price. ⁝ When we buy a car, we receive instructions for use. I will write them for you. They will be more comprehensive than just how to use the car itself (your life), but I will also include some traffic rules and explanations about other drivers (the environment) that you will encounter on your journey through life. ⁝ We learn and grow through other people in life. They are the people who get into your car. Some only travel part of the way, while others travel with you for a long time. You must realize that you are the one who opens the doors of your car and decides who and for how long they will ride with you. You have the right to reject them or kick them out of the car when you realize they're causing a distraction while driving. ⁝ One more important thing: From everyone you let into your car, you learn something. And when you understand their lesson, that

person either gets out of the car alone or you help them. Doing so allows you to make space for a new companion if you decide. But there's nothing wrong with traveling part of the way alone. It's also very refreshing and beneficial. ⋮ Anyone who enters your life can be a codriver or a passenger in the back seat. This means you are responsible for your success and happiness in life. There are no excuses. Ever. ⋮ If you feel like you're driving according to what others want, you haven't taken responsibility for your own life and you allow them to. You can't let anyone take the steering wheel out of your hands. Let them sit in their own car and drive it however they want. ⋮ You'll probably switch cars many times in life. It all depends on your current needs, desires, and abilities. In one period, you might prefer sports cars; in another, family minivans or SUVs, and you may want to drive a limousine at the end. It

doesn't really matter. What's important is that the choice is yours and that you enjoy it. ⋮ We often drive too fast, can't predict situations, have trouble concentrating, and demand too much from our lives. ⋮ Accidents are great teachers—for those who are smart enough to learn from them. You will be calm and satisfied with your life when you realize that everything that happens or doesn't happen is for good. ⠿ Life is not always easy—but it is interesting. And copying from your neighbor usually doesn't help. Everyone writes their own manual. Every day anew. Every life situation is a story of its own. We become smarter from what we've experienced, not from what others tell us. ⠿

Writing this manual was one of the biggest challenges I've faced in life. For some, it might have been a walk in the park, but for me, I approached it with a bit of trepidation. You see, I've always lived with the belief (and still do) that I'm not a good writer. I felt like my brother and I had divided our skills—he wrote, and I did the math. One day, a friend asked me, »Who told you that you can't write?« I couldn't remember. Maybe no one did. But that's beside the point. I've always admired people who can effortlessly express their thoughts in writing. Whenever I had to write something, I would ask someone better for help. And if you avoid doing something, you can't improve. It's as simple as that. ⋮ I met Svitlana Buko in 2015, a week after she arrived in Slovenia. We hit it off, and I became her »teacher« of Slovenian. During one of our meetings, she told me I should write a book. I almost fainted. Me? I don't have anything to say! And I can't even write! But Svitlana isn't one to give up easily. To prevent me from

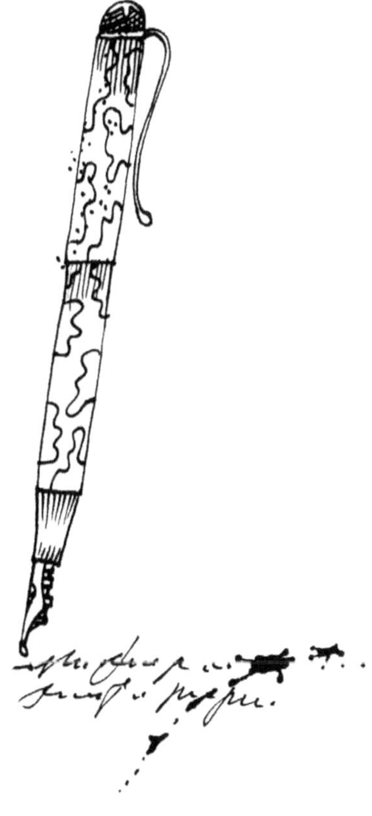

finding excuses, she gave me the book *Do You Want to Write a Book?* Somehow, she managed to push me in the right direction. I started thinking about what I could write and who it could be for. After a few failed ideas, I was inspired to write a manual for life. To overcome my fear, I decided to only publish it in two copies for my nieces. Writing for a large audience would scare me, but writing for my nieces would be manageable. And I started. ⋮ And here it is. I wrote it myself, without the help of anyone better than me. Was it hard? Of course. Am I scared of criticism? No. I did the best I could at the time, and it will have to suffice. ⋮ I'm grateful to Svitlana for pushing me into this, and I'm thankful to myself for accepting the challenge and overcoming one of my biggest fears. ⋮ We must surround ourselves with people who believe in us and encourage us. Only then can we go higher and further. We can push past our limits and achieve things we never thought were possible. ⁙

As I've come to realize, I need to tackle my beliefs to change my life. Our beliefs define us, and therefore they shape our experiences. When we believe in something, we act as if it were true. Whether we think we can do something or not, we're right either way. ⋮ Change is scary, especially when it comes to our beliefs. But the truth is, are we the same people today with the same beliefs as yesterday, a year ago, five years ago? Our beliefs are essential, especially those about ourselves and our abilities. They can either support or hinder us in achieving what we want. Our beliefs are personal and often mistaken. ⋮ So what is a belief? A belief is a truth as we understand it to be. It's a statement we make to ourselves and consider to be absolute truth, and this statement then governs our lives. ⋮ Our beliefs serve as the foundation for our actions in life and influence every aspect of it. They affect the way we think and see ourselves, others, and the world; the goals we have; and the decisions we make in daily situations. ⋮ We must first be aware of ourselves and our limitations to improve our lives. Our beliefs guide our lives. We experience what we believe and then say, »I knew it would be like that!« But it happened that way because we were directing energy toward that scenario. ⋮ Our beliefs are strongly influenced by our society and culture, and many of our core beliefs are formed in childhood. By reaching adulthood, we already have many beliefs that stay with us for the rest of our lives. Many people give up a chance to try something they don't believe in, but experience is needed to improve life. That's why we are where we are and progress at a less-than-desirable pace. ⋮ Our beliefs determine our attitudes, judgments, and perceptions and have incredible power. Based on our beliefs, we differentiate between good and bad, right and wrong. They define our relationships, moral values, education, sexuality, career choices, ethical principles, and attitude toward money. ⫶ But beliefs are not self-evident, not sent from heaven, and not unchanging. They are a matter of choice. We can change our beliefs and create a life that aligns with our values and desires. Don't let your beliefs limit you. Embrace the power to change and design the life you want. ⫶⫶

At the age of forty-two, I burned out. But I didn't realize it at the time. Even doctors couldn't figure out what was wrong with me, so I had to visit many specialists, which required much time and patience. ⦂ While waiting for one of these exams, I met an older woman who made a big impression on me and helped me come to an important realization. I knocked on the doctor's door, and before it opened, the waiting woman said to me, »You won't pass me, will you?« »No, of course not,« I hurried to answer. »I'm just going to ask if I'm in the right place.« The woman calmed down and complained that she had been waiting for exams all morning and was very tired and hungry. She mentioned that she had to leave home very early because she had to transfer several city buses. The chat developed, the word turned to life, and the woman was exceptional. Very wise, full of humor, and highly sensible. ⦂ We finished the exams simultaneously, and I offered to take her home. She was happy and surprised at the same time. The journey to her house was unforgettable—we had fun and laughed. We simply had a great time. She explained that she lives alone, cooks for herself daily, and makes excellent dumplings that I must try. ⦂ The drive went by too quickly, and when she asked me if we would ever see each other again, my thoughts were already elsewhere, at work, and the obligations that awaited me were buzzing in my head ... I told her we would see each other again and wished her good health and a beautiful day. ⦂ When I got to work, it struck me how foolishly I had behaved. I said goodbye with one of those cliches—»See you.« Without information, without a specific agreement, without ... She only knew my name. I felt lousy. ⦂ For a few days, I was tormented by acting so thoughtlessly, and I thought about how to fix it. So, I took action. The next day, I drove to the apartment building where I had left the woman and checked the address. Then I looked through the phone book for the names of the residents. I knew she lived alone, which meant her phone number would be listed under her name in the phone book. Given that she was over ninety, I imagined her name was quite traditional (like Mary or Anne). I called in the morning when retirees were usually at home. And I found her. The first person I called was the right one. Mrs. Mary. Imagine her surprise on the other end of the phone! I explained how and why I embarked on the search. I gave her my phone number to call me if she needed help. ⋮ Unfortunately, I never met with the woman again, but she will always remain in my memory as someone who helped me become a better person. ⋮ Being attentive means you care. It means you are focused on the moment and the person with you. Your thoughts don't wander off in different directions. You don't let distractions around you get in the way. You direct your attention to your conversation partner. You listen more than you talk. ⋮ Being attentive is a quality that is essential for building and maintaining good relationships between partners, friends, colleagues—and oneself. Attention must be sincere. It requires focus. ⋮ This means noticing things you wouldn't usually see when your mind is too preoccupied with the future or the past, thinking about what needs to be done, or reflect-

ing on what you have done. ⋮ There is nothing worse than attention shown out of politeness. If you want to evoke genuine sympathy in people, let them know that you are happy to see them. The feeling of importance is precious. The person you make feel this way will never forget it. ⋮ The art of living is to live attentively in the present. We must be aware of every moment. ⁞

Many years ago, I completely froze on stage in front of a large audience. My entire speech disappeared from my mind, and I struggled to get out a few confused words. It was one of the most challenging moments of my life. ⋮ Why did this happen? ⋮ Because I hadn't experienced or processed certain things the way I should have. A few days before the event, my father passed away. I convinced myself that it would be best for me to cope by working. I worked even harder than usual, acting as if nothing had happened. I felt a deep heartache but didn't acknowledge it—I suppressed it and tried to forget it. This worked for a while, but I didn't realize that the pain remained and still affected me ... Suppressed and unprocessed emotions have a tendency to resurface eventually. And not only that—they often appear at the most inappropriate times and in the most unpleasant ways, intending to make us remember them and learn from them. And I did. Nothing can be avoided. ⋮ The sooner you face your pain or problem, the easier it is to resolve. The longer you wait, the harder it becomes. And above all, you don't know when and in what form the »lesson« will appear. Indeed, we will not be prepared. It always surprises us. ⋮ Our body calms and relax when we understand emotions, accept their message, and follow their instructions. The most common obstacle to adulthood is the inability to accept sadness and grieving. ⋮ The primary purpose of emotions is to convey information. About oneself. About others. About others to oneself. There are only two emotions, pleasure and pain—whether the feeling is good or hurts. Whatever we do in life, we do it for two reasons: to avoid pain or experience pleasure. ⋮ Anger and joy are the only fundamental emotions that fill us with healthy energy. It makes us active and creative. If we reject anger, we reject energy. We must allow ourselves to be angry without condemning our emotions. Anger always means something needs to change. ⋮ Emotions are just energy, and all energy can be transformed. Confronting what we run from is never pleasant. Feeling these emotional states is not what we want, but it is what we need. ⋮ When we become emotionally mature, we allow others to have different opinions. We understand that our emotions are not a reflection of others' actions but rather a reflection of our own beliefs. We take responsibility for our emotions and stop blaming others for our feelings. ⁝

Dragan and I had a cat named Lion, known for his unique expression of emotions. When we went on a one-week vacation, we ensured he was well cared for. A lady named Marta brought him food every day. And not just any food, but gourmet meals that Lion loved. Marta was a cat lover and took great care of him. She cooked him chicken and other goodies he adored. His soul was also taken care of. She read to him daily (I don't know what) and pampered him in various ways. ⋮ Upon our return, Lion acted as if he was happy to see us. He didn't show resentment as he usually did, and it seemed he didn't hold it against us for leaving him alone for a week. However, it was different. He disappeared into the upper floor at some point, and a deathly silence set in. Dragan immediately suspected something was wrong. He went to check and found that Lion had pooped in the middle of our bed. To hurt us, he couldn't have found a better place. ⋮ The sight made Dragan very angry, while I laughed. Of course, I was not indifferent and was mad at Lion too. But he could hardly show his indigna-

tion more clearly. His message was clear: »I'm angry because you left me alone, and I had to let you know somehow.« Since he couldn't express it with words, he chose a very effective way. ⋮ People usually express their emotions in three ways: through conversation with another person, writing, or physical expression (such as crying, breaking dishes, etc.). ⋮ It doesn't matter what we choose from the list above. What's important is that we do something. We have to let others know that their words or actions have stirred up certain emotions within us. This way, we process and get rid of them. ⁙

One of the most beautiful and unique birthday gifts I've ever received was from my dear friend Beba. She offered to host a birthday party for me, taking care of everything from start to finish. She was a fantastic hostess, and we had an unforgettable evening. ⦂ Don't rush to the nearest store for inspiration when thinking about what to give someone and grab something at the nearest convenience store that fits your budget before the last minute. ⦂ If we care about someone, we must make an effort. We must consider what will make them happy or what they need most. Plan ahead and be open to ideas. It's not all about money. Some things require time, good intentions, and a lot of love. Put in the effort to create something yourself. Bake a cake, write a poem, or plan a trip. A great gift doesn't have to cost much, if anything. ⦂⦂

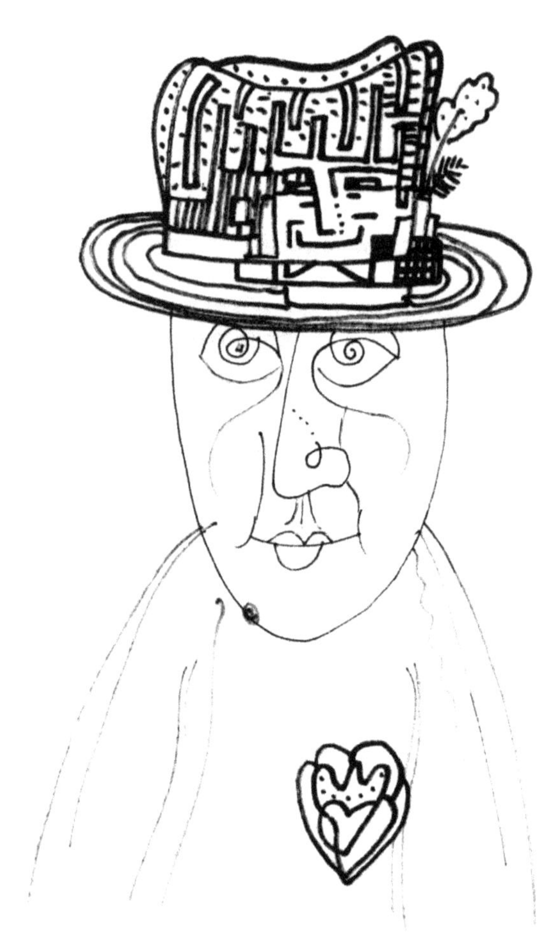

What to buy for a man's sixtieth birthday? Men are supposedly simple creatures, easy to please. But for such a milestone, it deserved something extra special. After much consideration, I came up with the idea of throwing a surprise party and gifting him a newspaper filled with contributions from people who have been a part of his life at various stages—schoolmates, college friends, colleagues, basketball teammates, family, and photography and music peers. ⋮ Collecting contributions was a unique challenge. Some were easier to get than others, but I managed them all with persistence. It was an enjoyable period during which I got to know many new people from Dragan's »past« life. The project took up a significant portion of my schedule, spanning six months with varying intensities. ⋮ I had a team of helpers who made this project possible.

FROM THE NEWSPAPER: »LIFE WITH DRAGAN IS LIKE LIVING IN A MIXED SEASON WITHOUT A WEATHER FORECAST. YOU NEVER KNOW WHAT'S COMING, NEVER GET BORED BECAUSE IT CHANGES TOO QUICKLY, BUT IT TAKES A LOT OF ENERGY AND ADAPTABILITY.« MARJANA

A
B

We scoured names and addresses of people Dragan hadn't seen in over forty years, some I had never met. They were all thrilled with the idea and eagerly participated. I enjoyed receiving their contributions—some wrote, some drew, but all shared their perspectives and experiences with Dragan, which I had never known before. Each person had a unique experience with him, and we all had one thing in common—we knew and loved Dragan. ⋮ The highlight was when all the »creators« came together at the surprise party and presented the final product to him. Priceless. ⋮ This project reminded me that the journey is as important as the destination. In my case, the journey lasted six months, and I enjoyed every moment, met new people, and learned a lot. ⁞

It all started in 1996 when I set out to find the perfect black jacket. Not too expensive, fancy, or sporty, suitable for everyday wear and special occasions. A jacket that's hard to describe to your partner, who kindly offers to help you search for it. ⋮ Dragan wasn't known for his patience, but that day he exceeded himself. After a few hours and countless kilometers walking the streets of Cologne, I suggested he wait for me in a friendly local pub over a beer instead. At first, he rejected the idea and continued to accompany me, but in the end, he gave in. Enough is enough. After all those countless inspected jackets, he couldn't understand what I was looking for. ⋮ When I finally joined him at the pub, exhausted, he couldn't believe his eyes. I had come back without a perfect black jacket. ⋮ We often don't know what we want, but we know exactly what we don't want. And that's how it was with the jacket. But then there comes a moment when you see the right one (also applies to men). There's chemistry; who knows. I had to wait a little longer for the chemistry with the black jacket. It didn't happen in Cologne, but a week later in Klagenfurt. It was love at first sight. ⋮ In life, we often appreciate things more that we had to work harder to get. And that's how the

black jacket had a special status. ⋮ It is often said that you should get rid of clothes you don't wear for a year or two. Maybe, but how can I say goodbye to a jacket I had such a hard time finding? Instead of removing the jacket, I put it in a special place in my closet. And that's where my friend noticed it when she came to visit. It was love at first sight (for the second time). I sensed it was time that the black jacket got a new life, that someone who really wanted it and would appreciate it and wear it should have it. I gave it to my friend for her fiftieth birthday. She was delighted. ⋮ It's great if we know what we want. Sometimes we need a lot of determination and patience to figure it out. But it's worth it. I could have thrown in the towel back in Cologne and bought just any jacket, but I'm sure it wouldn't have given me so much happiness. And this story wouldn't exist. ⁞

When Dragan's niece Alja announced her wedding a few years ago, I immediately began brainstorming what to give the newlyweds. I find it most fulfilling to participate in creating a gift and prefer original gifts that cannot be bought, so my ideas went in that direction. ⋮ I remembered Dragan's aunt Bojana, a legendary cook who had written down many recipes. Alja also enjoyed cooking, and I decided this was the way. I presented the idea to Dragan, his brother Bojan, and Bojan's wife Zlata (Alja's parents) to prepare dishes using Bojana's recipes, take photographs, write down the recipes, and publish a family cookbook. The idea was well received, and we got to work. ⋮ We frequently met for a couple of months, sifted through old recipes, cooked, took photos, and enjoyed each other's company. When the dishes weren't photogenic enough, we ate them and repeated the process enthusiastically. ⋮ Our family cookbook was more than just any cookbook. It had a greater mission of preserving our family's culinary heritage, a collection of recipes for the kind of food that we used to love and still enjoy today. The cookbook included recipes from long ago up to the 1980s. Zlata and I, the next generation, added a few of our favorite recipes. ⋮ In our case, the saying »in unity is power« was true and was also fun and delicious. ⋮⋮

VINUM
SPUMA
ALOIS

Friendship is essential to our lives, providing us with meaning and purpose. In true friendships, the law of attraction applies. We choose our friends based on who we are, our way of thinking, and how we respond to the world around us. True friends never judge or condemn us, and we reciprocate the same kindness toward them. They offer a shoulder to cry on and objectively tell us when we've made a mistake, even if it might upset us. ⋮ We choose friends with similar interests, desires, and perspectives on things that matter to us. However, creating friendships comes with a certain level of risk. We reveal our personalities, and our new friends do the same. Our new friend might not like us, or the opposite might happen. The friendship could become cool and eventually come to an end. We have all experienced such a process of alienation at least once. ⋮ True friends hold up a mirror to us in the most precious way. They don't judge us but constructively and critically tell us when we've made a mistake. We can do the same thing when they stray and don't have to fear losing the friendship. Friendship is a delicate category that provides meaning to our existence. ⋮ Alma Karlin said, »Everyone who crosses our path is our teacher who knowingly or unknowingly forms our character. Thus, we may compare our soul with a passport in which everyone who has touched our fate has left their visa or stamp. ⋮

We cannot do without shoes. The same is true of friends. So what's the similarity between the two? ⠿ Of course, we don't just have one pair of shoes. We have shoes for various events and for different seasons. We wear some for hiking, the beach, work, parties, and various sports. When do we change them? When we get tired of them or wear them out or they become too tight. ⠿ Just like shoes, we have multiple friends. We go to the theater with some, to sporting events with others, out to eat with others, and on vacation with others … ⠿ How do we buy shoes? Sometimes too fast, sometimes with forethought, sometimes just to comfort ourselves. When we are young, we have a lot of new shoes because we quickly grow out of them. Is that hard for us? Mostly not. We look forward to having a new pair of shoes and can hardly wait to find a reason to buy one. Some people are willing to pay a lot for shoes, some not.

Shoes mean a lot to some people, which is why they care for them, and to others, they mean very little. Such people buy cheap shoes, don't take care of them, and get rid of them quickly and buy new ones.

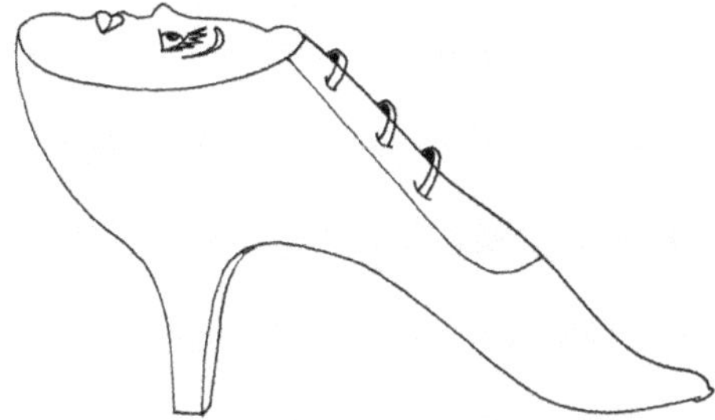

They are careless with their purchases, and they often buy shoes that are not quite right or are uncomfortable. ⦙ We similarly make friendships. Sometimes too fast, sometimes passing up good ones. Some people are prepared to do much for friends, and some too little. Some cultivate friendships, and others are amazed when friends abandon them. ⦙ It's the same with both shoes and friends. Sooner or later, we get new ones when we grow out of the old ones or if they no longer suit our current image. With shoes, it is the outside image; with friends the inside. And there is no reason to feel bad about it. We should always try to be in tune with ourselves and to feel good. Sometimes to feel good, we need a new pair of shoes, sometimes a new friend, and sometimes both. And sometimes, it's fun to run around barefoot. ⁞

How would I describe the relationship between spouses or partners? Imagine the mechanism of a cog wheel, how perfectly the wheels fit into each other. Such a machine can run for years. Then all of a sudden, the gears get worn out, and they don't grip anymore. They don't turn. They stall in place. Cogwheels must be constantly oiled; if not, they get dull and don't function. Likewise, if we want to have a good relationship, we have to work on it constantly. ⦂ In life, we need not only a partner but also a fellow traveler. We do not look for the perfect partner. We do not look for the ideal partner. We look for the most suitable, the most compatible. A kindred spirit that brings out the best in us. ⦂ To achieve harmony in life, we need the courage to see things as they are and the capacity to create an environment to our measure. When things change, it is always necessary to understand them in the new context: the way they are now, not under the influence of past experience and conclusions. We always need to learn new things and leave the old behind. ⦂ Healthy love is created between two people who recognize difficulties and find solutions together. We must make an effort in relationships and listen to our partners—sincerely, not just the words they say. Then we understand much more—not only about our partner but also ourselves. ⦂ Conflicts are alright. It is only vital that we know how to control and solve them. A relationship must be alive. Persistence in a relationship that doesn't make sense anymore is a waste of life. There is no point in persisting in a relationship where we no longer learn or grow. It is worse to be alone with someone who means a lot to you than to be alone with yourself. ⦂ In a healthy relationship, the boundaries between the two people are clear. When necessary, the partners can reject the other and accept rejection. People in healthy relationships with clear boundaries take responsibility for their values and problems, not their partner's values and issues. ⋮ You need two people for misunderstandings and conflicts, but you only need one to shut them down, the one who puts themselves first. Worrying too much about others makes it impossible to look at ourselves. Responsibility to ourselves does not only mean obligations; it also means rights. To be what we are, to feel what we feel, and to think what we think. ⋮ And one more annoying thing: what we don't solve in an old relationship will resurface in a new one. ⋮⋮

Let's talk about crossbars. No, not the ones used in pole vaulting—the ones we face when searching for a partner. The older we get, the higher the crossbar is set. But that's not necessarily a bad thing. ⋮ As we gain more life experience, we become more selective about the people we want to be with. We set our standards higher, demanding more from ourselves and potential partners. And that's a good thing. We owe it to ourselves to find someone who matches our values, desires, and ways of life. Of course, only some people are willing to work to jump over that high crossbar. But that's okay. They don't have to be in the competition. We shouldn't lower our standards just so someone can meet them. That's not fair to us, and it's not fair to them either. ⋮ So let's embrace the challenge of jumping over that high crossbar. Let's work on ourselves and demand the best from ourselves and our potential partners. And if someone who can't jump over it comes along, that's okay too. We'll find someone who can. Because when it comes to finding a partner, it's not about settling—it's about finding the perfect fit. ⸬

The first qualities we notice in others are often the most prominent in us. What irritates us about others and drives us up the wall simply reflects our inner beliefs that we need to change within ourselves. Instead of getting angry with others, we should be grateful that they have come into our lives as teachers, reminders of where we can grow and work on ourselves. ⋮ As relationships are two-way, we are only responsible for our part. We never need another person to make us better. When we understand this, we will stop asking others to change so that we can feel better. ⋮ Changing others is not productive. Everyone only changes if they choose to. The most we can do is influence them—by no longer participating in maintaining a state that does not require them to change. ⋮ When we change ourselves, we change our relationships. We start to attract different and new people into our lives. The more we love ourselves, the more we can love others. ⋮ If our well-being depends on improved behavior from others, we will face significant problems. At best, this is limiting, and at worst, it can be exhausting. When we understand that we have control over our own thoughts and emotions, we understand everything. ⋮ We should not put the responsibility for our lives into the hands of others. Instead of asking others to change their behavior, we should change our reaction to it. We cannot control their behavior, but we completely control our response. ⋮ We should not forget ourselves, hide behind others, surrender, or appease. No one can give us what we can give ourselves. ⋮ It is said that relationships are like a jug of milk. Sometimes we can put it back in the fridge in time. But if it is left out for too long and sours, there is nothing we can do to change it back into fresh milk. ⋮

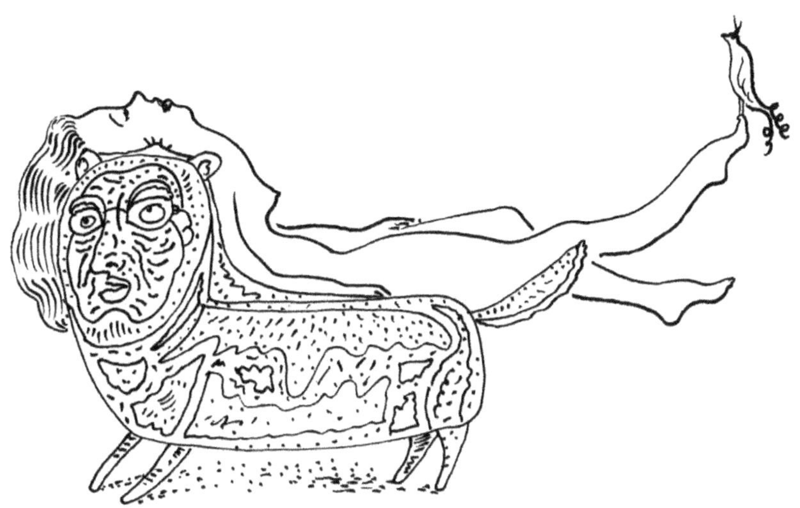

Agreement from others no longer means anything to us when we reach a certain level of self-realization. We need constructive criticism and someone with more knowledge, understanding, and experience. ⠿

A few years ago, I spent my vacation on Flores, an island between Bali and Australia. It doesn't matter for this story, but the point is that these places are entirely different from what we're used to in the West, with different cultures, customs, and traditions, yet so similar to ours. ⋮ As a tourist, I always blend in with the locals, talk to them, eat their food (if I can handle it), and attend local events. Fortunately, Flores is yet to be highly touristy. I traveled from the east to the island's west, from pure rural scenes to the more touristy west. I met many interesting locals and travelers on my journey. ⋮ My guide took me to a nightclub on the last night of our journey, which was said to be the best in Labuhanbatu. He introduced me to some of his acquaintances, we sat at a long table, and the evening passed by listening to the local band and drinking local beer. It struck me that we didn't talk much except for a few polite phrases and the exchange of basic information about where we were from. Everyone had their heads down, gazing at their phones, sending messages and photographs to each other, which I thought was unusual. I wondered if it was because most were about fifteen or twenty years younger than me. But that couldn't be the reason, because they also didn't speak among themselves. The scene was bizarre. ⋮ The reason is non-communication, which is one of the worst difficulties of our time. We exchange messages, but non-communication has become the rule. Our compassion and engagement with fellow human beings decline as we get lost in too much information. We communicate a lot, but our communication is too quick and superficial. Real communication takes time. True intimacy requires more than words—true intimacy means that we are available to others and can perceive if they are feeling well and prefer to

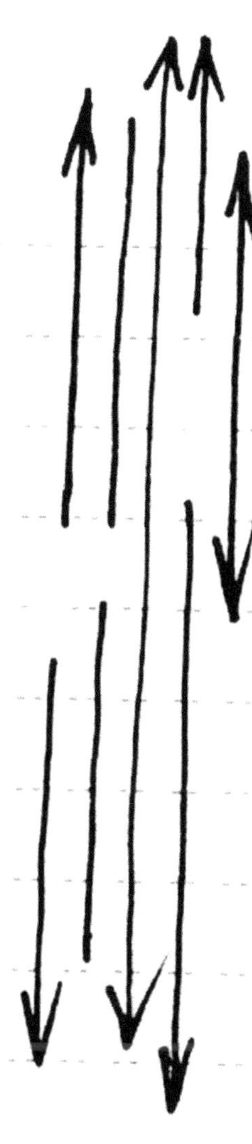

speak or be silent. ⋮ Communication gives life to a relationship. Just as breathing gives life to living beings, communication gives life to a relationship, allowing it to live, develop, and grow. Even if we don't want to communicate with someone, we've already sent them a message. ⋮ Through communication, we get to know other people—who they are and what they want—and we communicate to others who we are and what we want. Sensing the other person and their mood is very important for a relationship. In communication, we respond as we perceive it. The proper response at the right moment can make all the difference. The art of communication is in the balance between speaking and listening, asking and answering, and giving and receiving. ⋮ Let's take a moment to communicate better, be present for each other, and give each other the gift of our time and attention. Let's make a conscious effort to be there for each other, listen, and understand. Let's give each other the opportunity to feel heard, understood, and loved. Communication is the key to a better life and a better world. ⁞

Love sometimes means leaving. If you love someone, you let them go if that's what they desire or need, or leave them in a place of great enjoyment and go off alone. ⁝ When we moved out of our house, one of my most significant worries was what we would do with Bond. Bond is a cat with a big *C*. Intelligent, independent, playful, a tireless explorer of his surroundings, but always nearby when you need him. He was ten years old when we moved. I couldn't tear him away from his green surroundings and shut him up in an apartment. I simply couldn't take his freedom away. He needed it. I understood this and let it happen. I made an agreement with the new owners that Bond could stay in the house. Every so often, they send me pictures showing him enjoying himself on the couch, and my heart is overwhelmed. Neither of us would have been happy if I had taken him with me. Bond, because he would not be free, and I because I would have to watch him suffer. ⁝ To give love means to make it possible for others to be who they are. It is paradoxical: the more space we provide to our partner and the more we encourage our partner, the more the relationship will blossom. The more we try to limit our partner, the more we follow his every step or demand that we spend more time together, the more we contribute to discord in the relationship. ⁞

The subject of men and women is one of the most frequently debated themes. One area where the sexes differ is their brains. Often we believe men's are simple, women's complex. However, in her book *The Male Brain*, neuropsychiatrist Louann Brizendine offers a different picture. ⫶ She says that simplifying a male's brain to what lies below the belt is suitable for a joke, but it doesn't even start to reveal the entirety of the male brain. ⫶ The female and male brains have different ways of hearing, seeing, feeling, and evaluating what others are feeling. ⫶ Both men and women have a poor understanding of the fundamental biological and social impulses that motivate the opposite sex. In general, we do not realize the unseen effects of various genes, neurochemicals, and hormones. ⫶ In the book *The Female Brain*, Brizendine discusses the discovery that hormones have such a strong influence on the female brain that they actually create reality. She says that hormones shape the values and desires of women, influencing what they feel is important from day to day. Women feel the presence of hormones during all life phases. Every hormonal phase—childhood, adolescence, sexual maturity, motherhood, and menopause—has a specific chemical impact on various neurological connections responsible for thoughts, emotions, and interests. Brizendine writes that the level of hormones begins to fluctuate when girls are only three months old and continues after menopause, and that a woman's neurological reality is not as stable as a man's. Male neurological reality is like a mountain formed slowly and almost imperceptibly by glaciers, weather, and tectonic shifts over thousands of years. In contrast, female neurological reality is like the weather, constantly changing and difficult to predict. ⦂ But of course, we mustn't forget the heart. Neither women nor men can be strong if they ig-nore their emotions. ⦂ Sometimes men can be very hard to understand. Women as well. The more we learn about each other, the easier it will be to ac-cept the innate differences between the sexes. And, yes, long live our differenc-es! ⦂

Fortunately, I haven't had frequent contact with blackmailers. Two have crossed my path. I dealt with the first one quickly, but the second was a slightly more demanding sort and spent a little more time in my orbit, enriching my life experience. ⦂ You need two for blackmail, and all acts of blackmail have one thing in common: fear—fear of loss, fear of change, fear of rejection, fear of the loss of power. ⦂ By giving in to a blackmailer's demand, we actually teach them how to blackmail us. Each time we allow emotional blackmail, we lose contact with our integrity, the inner compass that helps us to define our values and behavior. Fear, obligation, and guilt are emotional conditions that blackmailers amplify in us. ⦂ One of the most interesting paradoxes of human behavior is that angry people who like to mete out punishment are, in reality, deeply frightened, but they rarely confront and deal with their own fears. Feeling threatened, they strike out against others to show their power. They cause so much suffering with their behavior that people usually leave them. Thus, their actions only serve to bring about what they fear most. ⦂ Most blackmailers believe that they are teaching us a really good lesson. Well, that's true once we learn it. When we allow pressure and discomfort to be exerted upon us, we reinforce bad behavior. The cruel truth is that when we allow someone to degrade our dignity and integrity, we are cooperating with them and helping them to harm us. ⦂ Emotional blackmail does not threaten our lives but takes away the most important thing—our personal integrity. Self-confident and stable people do not tyrannize others simply to prove their strength. ⦂⦂

I never saw myself as a perfectionist. It was others who pointed it out to me. I always thought that I wasn't good enough, and neither was anything I did. To me, perfectionists were people who did everything flawlessly. ⋮ I don't know if I was born a perfectionist or if it was the consequence of my upbringing—if I didn't get enough recognition from my parents when I did a good job, or maybe they just had different expectations. Almost all I ever heard from my father was what I did wrong. ⋮ It is certainly not easy to be a perfectionist. I had extremely high standards for myself. When I felt that I wouldn't be able to perform a specific task according to my expectations, I just didn't try to do it. This included foreign languages. I would rather not speak at all than make mistakes. ⋮ I also struggled with procrastination. It was never the right moment to start something new because I felt unprepared or needed to learn more. I spent more time on each task than necessary, perfecting every detail. I wanted everything to be perfect or not at all. My standards were so high that I simply couldn't reach them. I found myself in a vicious circle of exaggerated expectations and shooting for the top as if I were always trying to win a prize. ⋮ I remember once I came home from school, and my mother asked me how my day was.

»It was okay,« I said. »How was your reading?« she asked. »Fine, I was second,« I told her. Then she asked who was first, followed by my surprising answer—»No one.« »What do you mean, no one?« she questioned. »No one was the best, and I was the second best.« I was in the first grade of primary school. I was already burdened with the idea that I had to be the best and be perfect for earning praise. ⋮ I had a lot of trouble with stage fright because I had high standards and was convinced I wasn't prepared enough to do a task excellently. I couldn't differentiate between what was the best and what was good enough. ⋮ I kept working harder and harder, not knowing how to set limits. As a result, I was increasingly exhausted, which led to decreased productivity. I was always anxious, stressed, and burdened with whether I could improve things. This eventually broke me down and led to burnout. Fortunately, I didn't suffer grave consequences, but the warning was serious enough that I took it to heart. I learned to take care of myself, developed a more healthy level of egotism, and learned to say no. What a relief! ⋮ Discovering that I'm okay and don't have to be perfect to love myself has been a game-changer. Even if I spend a day in bed and don't do all my workouts and other »essential« things perfectly, I still love and accept myself. I know when and for what purpose perfectionism is valuable and necessary and when and where I can be just myself. I know it is enough to breathe, like myself, and enjoy life. ⋮ I have optimized my work to such a degree that I am satisfied with what I produce, and at the same time, I have managed to somewhat lower my standards. However, that is not always the case. Sometimes I still complicate matters and spend too much time sorting things out. But I am improving. ⋮ I have accepted that I am a fallible and imperfect being with flaws. Life became much easier when I realized that others expect less from me than I demand of myself. Now I know that I am all right the way I am, though that does not mean that everything I do is all right. ⋮ Perfection is the enemy of performance. It is better to do something, even if it has flaws, than to wait for perfection and lose time, momentum, and opportunity. ⋮ *»If I waited for perfection, I would never write a word«* Margaret Atwood ⁞

Self-esteem is what we believe about ourselves—how we see ourselves. Our self-perception is shaped and developed from childhood. We learn both healthy and unhealthy patterns. As adults, we behave in accordance with our beliefs, expectations, and inner faith and the idea we have of ourselves. ⋮ Positive self-esteem means that we are able to accept ourselves with all our positive and negative traits. Confidence gives us the courage to take on challenges and live life fully. It's a quality that can be gained or lost. Self-esteem and confidence together form self-respect. ⋮ Self-respect can be learned; it's a discipline of the mind, a habit of the reason that can never be faked. It's something we are responsible for and has nothing to do with how others see us or our reputation, which brave people don't need. Our power lies in taking responsibility for our lives and thus gaining self-respect. ⋮ To have a good relationship with ourselves means that we recognize our uniqueness, do not care about the expectations of others, and live in accordance with our own desires. ⁞

One of my biggest misconceptions was that mistakes are not allowed for adults. I always feared people would laugh at me if I made a silly »mistake.« As a child, I wasn't allowed to make mistakes, and as an adult, I didn't allow myself to make them. That was my belief. ⁞ Fortunately, I've learned a lot from my mistakes. I realized I'll miss out on good things if I don't take risks. I learned that I shouldn't be afraid to make mistakes but be fearful of not making them. I learned that I can only learn something or grow if I make mistakes. I realized that mistakes are part of the learning process, that there's nothing wrong with them, and that they're not a sign of defeat. ⁞ Now I know it's easier to recognize other people's mistakes than my own. I now know that mistakes are a vital component of growth and change in life and that I can only learn one way—through action. I also understand that the fundamental mistake is to stop trying. ⁞ In my youth, I rarely understood what became evident in my mature years: There's always something to learn, and mistakes are our best teachers, so they're allowed. They're proof that we're taking risks, and taking risks leads to innovation and creative ideas. ⁞ I'm no longer afraid of mistakes. I make them and will continue to make them! But I strive not to repeat them. I use each mistake to my advantage, and I've never learned so quickly as I do now. I know I'm doing something wrong if I don't make any mistakes. ⁞ Self-confidence is a valuable resource for a good life. When we trust ourselves in life, we can live in touch with ourselves, make our own decisions, and not be afraid of the burden of making mistakes. Only then can we freely create. Only then does life become wonderful, not experienced in constant fear. ⁞ We must respect people as they are. And if they make a mistake, we must allow them to make it. ⁞⁞

Everything happens for a reason. Even eagles need to be pushed out of the nest to fly, as David McNally writes: ⋮ The eagle draws courage from its innate wisdom. Until its offspring discover their wings, their lives lack purpose. They won't understand that they are privileged to be born as eagles until they learn to soar. The greatest gift you can give them is to push them out of the nest. That is the highest act of love. And so, one by one, she pushed them over the edge. And they flew! ⋮ We all have wings—wings of wisdom, creativity, and inspiration. We all can fly. But first, we must discover our wings. ⋮ Courage grows just like a muscle, becoming stronger with each use. Courage isn't the opposite of fear. The opposite of fear is love. ⠿

I've always been a responsible person. I've taken responsibility even when someone else should have taken the reins. Call it naivety, inexperience, or foolishness. ⋮ Responsibility has two sides. Some people avoid it, while others take on too much. Responsibility isn't handed to us on a silver platter. Like everything else, it's something we need to learn. ⋮ Taking complete responsibility for our lives means we don't make excuses or blame others for what's not working. When we take responsibility, we feel a sense of personal power. ⁞

Stepping into the world of parenting can be a daunting task. After all, it's one of the most challenging jobs, and no one has prepared you for it. Some people are naturally better at it, while others struggle to find their footing. And the fear of doing more harm than good to your children is always present. ⠿ Perhaps that's the reason why I never decided to have a child. Maybe it was because I didn't feel mature enough to handle such a big responsibility. Whatever. The decision was mine, and I have never regretted it. ⠿ Now I know that we can also be a parent to ourselves. We can be the kind of parents we wish we had if only our parents could have been. And I've learned that if we want our children to love and accept themselves, we must first love and accept ourselves. To raise confident and brave children, we can't scare, shame, blame, or judge them. We learn empathy and connectedness—the two things that give our lives meaning and purpose—by experiencing them. ⠿ I had to spend time on myself, not my children, to understand all this. And now, I know why I made the decision I did. I can use my knowledge to be the best aunt I can be. ⠿

I loved and highly respected my father, but he had this annoying habit of trying to manage the lives of others. He had a clear plan for everyone's future, including mine. The problem was that I also had a clear plan of what I did and didn't want. My father's values were, in contrast to my own, traditional and patriarchal, and it was inevitable that our values would clash when it came to ideas about *my* life. ⋮ I idealized my father as a young girl and fought for his attention and praise. I wanted to prove that I was trustworthy and capable of achieving the same things as boys, even wishing I were born a boy. I preferred male company and found girl activities boring. ⋮ My father often held up my classmates as examples for me to follow, as they met his expectations. In my teenage years, I realized I couldn't meet his expectations and chose my own path. I wasn't sure what I wanted then, but I knew I wanted to stay true to myself. ⋮ In my family, work was highly valued but not intellectual creation. My father appreciated practical people who could create something useful with their hands. There's nothing wrong with that, but it's not the only valuable thing. ⋮ What was expected of women was also clear: marriage, at least two children, and weekly church attendance. ⋮ I had the courage and perseverance to live my life the way I chose. I'm still amazed that I, a tiny little thing, had the bravery to tell him that. I'm proud of myself for overcoming my fear. ⋮ All of this made me the person I am today. I escaped from everything that suffocated me and started enjoying things that matter to me. I love traveling, socializing, enjoying life, having beautiful things, reading, and learning. I like to show affection, give gifts, and be alone with myself. I need freedom and love it. I never got married. I love living. I love being a woman. ⋮ We must know who we are and what we want and live accordingly. We must trust that everything will be okay and that we have made the right choices. We must embrace our independence and be confi-dent and productive in our decisions. ⁞

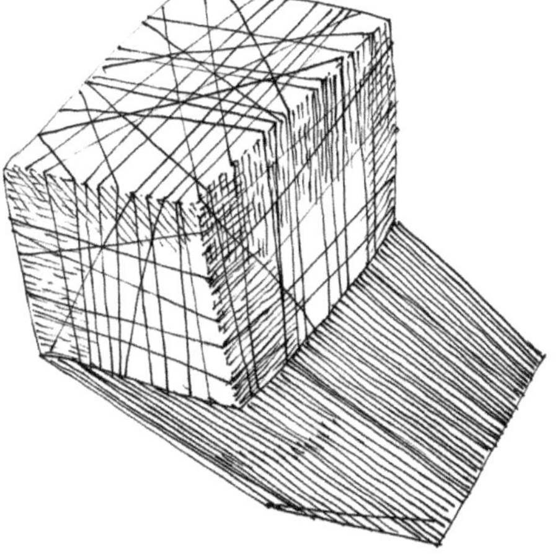

»You'll always make your own decisions, which is good! I'm happy that you're happy.« That's what I wish I had heard from my father. Although I know he wanted to say it, I never heard it. ⦂ Sometimes we have to make decisions that may not be pleasant at the moment but are beneficial in the long run. If we don't decide to pursue our dreams, our fears will become a reality. We create and see what we expect to see. The results will also be negative if we approach something with negative preconceptions. We create our own reality. In the end, we only regret opportunities we didn't take, relationships we were too afraid to have, and decisions we didn't make soon enough. ⦂ Having a true feeling when making decisions and doing things is essential, regardless of what others see as important or what is objectively wise. ⦂ We must never delay important decisions. It's best to face them when they arise. It's important not to procrastinate with unpleasant tasks and not to sweep them under the rug. It's like a snowball. At first, it's small and manageable, but if we let it go, it will roll and get bigger and bigger with each passing moment. It will be big and uncontrollable when it finally reaches the valley, and its destructive power will be unpredictable. ⦂⦂

I have always felt uncomfortable when I was dependent on someone. It can be very exhausting at times, but it's worth it. I simply can't handle feelings of dependency. I can't stand someone else controlling my time. I'm willing to compromise and adapt, but only when my freedom isn't threatened. I am ready to pay a high price for this feeling. It may be costly, but it's sweet. ⋮ Independence requires courage. We have to be brave enough to reject what we don't want with a smile and without excuses. No one or nothing has any power over us; we are the masters of our thoughts. If we can't align and balance them, it will also reflect in our lives. We are solely responsible for our actions. ⋮ If we take care of ourselves, we seem more pleasant to others, and we are happier as well. We don't have to suffer. We live much more easily if we don't expect anything from others. If we don't feel comfortable in our own company, it's possible that others won't appreciate it either. People demand happiness from others that they cannot create. ⋮ Only when we don't demand anything from others, don't regret anything, and have nothing to lose can neither people nor situations affect us. We can find unlimited sources of strength within ourselves. And as such, we are very annoying to others. No one can scare or control us. ⁞

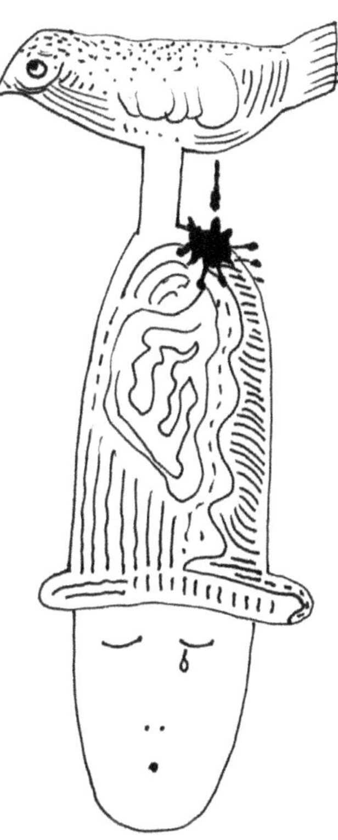

Coincidences are messages that guide our actions and allow our dreams and intentions to come to light. ⋮ No random occurrence is insignificant. Coincidences are messages about the miraculous potential of every moment, and if we understand the forces that shape them, we can start changing our lives. ⋮ A change in even the slightest detail, attributed to »coincidence,« could result in us being in a completely different place, surrounded by different people, working a different job, and following a different path in life. And this book might be completely different, or it might not even exist. ⋮⋮

Failing isn't a reflection of a task's unsolvability; it's a reflection of our approach to solving it. So when we face failure, it's an opportunity to re-evaluate our strategies, fine-tune our techniques, and persevere with a renewed sense of purpose. ⦂ Embrace failure as a chance to learn, grow, and succeed. The more you fail, the closer you are to achieving your goals. So trust yourself, be persistent, and never give up. ⦂ Slovenian former cross-country skier Petra Majdič astutely observed, *»I believe that if you haven't achieved your goal—you either didn't persist long enough or you didn't try enough times.«*

A JOURNEY TO MASTERY

Growing up, my parents taught me the value of acquiring practical skills. My mother was a master seamstress who always shared her knowledge with others with great patience. At seventeen, she finally convinced me to try my hand at sewing. Of course, we both had different expectations. As an experienced woman, my mother knew that acquiring sewing skills required a lot of practice and patience. But at that age, I was in a hurry for everything. ⦂ I approached the project enthusiastically, rushing to the store and buying three types of silk with my scholarship money, ready for a new challenge. My mother shook her head and tried to explain to me that I should approach this more carefully, with materials that wouldn't be a waste. She advised me to use an old garment or sheet as learning material, which seemed like a complete waste of my precious time. My theory was that I would work harder if I had materials in my hands that I had paid a lot of money for, and I would make something useful for myself. »Nothing should go to waste,« said Pippi Longstocking, my childhood idol. And I agreed with her ultimately. My time was too precious to be wasted on making clothes for plastic dolls. ⋮ I imagined I would walk out of the house the next day in a beautiful silk shirt, perfectly tailored and sewn by me. Well, it was more complicated. I did learn how to sew, but not in one day. It was very educational, and I realized that the size of each masterpiece is only recognized when you tackle it yourself or delve into it deeply. When we know we can do something, we are on the path to mastery. ⋮ Determination, action, self-belief, and perseverance are the virtues that lead us to success. However, we must realize that mastery requires time, energy, a lot of practice, self-discipline, and patience. The biggest pitfall we can fall into in life is impatience. With impatience and restlessness, we punish ourselves. We create stress, dissatisfaction, and fear within ourselves. ⋮ Let's be optimistic and learn from the best. Let's do the best we can until we know better. When we know better, let's do better. Very few desires are fulfilled on their own without hard work and sacrifice. ⠿

ABOUT PROCRASTINATION

In the previous chapter, I talked about mastery. In this chapter, I can proudly say that at some point in my life, I became a master of procrastination. Perfectionism and fear played a significant role in acquiring this title. ⋮ Nothing changes if nothing changes. For most people, procrastination is a way to avoid fully living in the present moment. We often wait our entire lives to start really living. In reality, we regret the things we didn't do more than the things we did. ⋮ If we're unhappy, we have three options: Remove ourselves from the situation, change it, or fully accept it. If we want to take responsibility for our lives, we must choose one of these three options and accept the consequences that come with it. ⋮ We're never 100 percent ready for change, so waiting for the perfect conditions is pointless. It just means we lack the courage to take action. I had the theory down but needed more courage. And when we make excuses for why now isn't the right time to do something, we display incredible creativity. ⋮ *The secret of getting ahead is getting started. The secret of getting started is breaking your complex overwhelming tasks into small manageable tasks and starting on the first one.* *—Mark Twain* ⁞

THE JOY OF DISCOVERING
NEW KNOWLEDGE

Learning is a never-ending journey, and it's okay if we don't know everything. Sometimes, when we ask someone how to do something, we get the answer: »It's easy!« But it's not always that simple. What's easy for one person can be a nightmare for someone else. ⋮ Once, my mom offered me some cottage cheese to make burek. I wasn't thrilled about the idea, as I had no clue how to make it. And then came that »it's easy« response. You make a stretchy dough . . . Stretchy dough? I had never made it before, and even other types of dough made me nervous. I decided to take the cottage cheese but buy the dough. My mom was quite upset with the idea, and on the way home, I thought it over and decided to make the dough myself. I figured it couldn't be that hard. ⋮ My household needed to be better equipped with small appliances at that time. No food processors, no dough mixers . . . So, I tackled it by hand. But first, I went through all the cookbooks and checked out recipes online . . . and in the end, I was pretty confused. Some recipes had eggs, others didn't, and it was often mentioned to add this or that ingredient to taste! The worst part was that I didn't even know what consistency

I needed to achieve for the dough to stretch nicely. ⋮ After my research, I got to work. To taste, of course. Things went from bad to worse. The result was a compact mass that showed no signs of stretching. The unsuccessful product went into the trash. I decided to buy the dough from the market the next day. ⋮ The woman who I bought it from looked at me quite skeptically. She sensed that I wasn't skilled in this task and tried to help me. When I asked how many sheets I needed, I looked at her helplessly and explained that I had half a kilo of cottage cheese and had no idea how much dough I needed. Then came the question of whether I would roll or layer the burek. I decided to roll it, and the expression on her face indicated that she doubted my rolling abilities. She advised me to make the burek in layers. And I did. It was excellent. ⋮ But this dough story wouldn't leave me alone. I decided to learn about it. The female team I spend a week with on the island of Vis every year was perfect for taking me into the world of stretchy dough making. I had a blast learning and enjoyed the goodies we made with our combined efforts all week long. ⋮ It's not embarrassing if we don't know how to do something. If we can't reach the desired knowledge on our own, we can ask for help. Empowerment comes from taking the initiative to learn and grow. So let's embrace our curiosity, have fun, and keep learning! ⁞

PERSISTENCE PAYS OFF

A few years ago, when I was fifty-three, I took on a unique challenge. I started getting bored with my usual fitness routine and needed a new spark. I decided to learn how to do a handstand without pushing off. A younger colleague showed me a training program she used to meet this challenge. It didn't seem too difficult, and I planned to try it in the gym that same afternoon. She looked at me skeptically and explained that the training was highly demanding and would take at least a year of effort for me to master it. This was coming from a twenty-six-year-old who was taking her personal trainer exam! ⦂ But it didn't scare me. I confidently told my trainer about my plan at the gym. He was taken aback. He quickly tried to discourage me, saying that it was an incredibly demanding exercise and that I should try something easier and more appropriate for me instead, like a backstroke or a marathon. Ha, right! Whenever someone tells me something is too hard or impossible, I get even more motivated to try it. So instead of discouraging, he motivated me. I asked him, in his opinion, if it was possible for me at my fitness level and age to achieve this goal. He confirmed that it was possible and added that he would run naked across the town from the gym to the city center (about 6 km) if I could perform the exercise in less than a year. What a deal! ⦂ I immediately started my training. A whole group of people who witnessed our conversation became my fans and encouraged and cheered me throughout my training at the gym. Maybe the naked part had something to do with it. After a year of training, we all gathered to the determine if I could meet my challenge. Unfortunately, according to my trainer, I did not manage to perform the exercise completely flawlessly, as I slightly pushed off where I shouldn't. So my trainer, to the disappointment of my supporters, did not run naked across the town. Oh well. I proved that with persistence, we can achieve a lot and inspire many others along the way. ⦂ Everything happens gradually. We can't skip steps, and rushing without a plan is pointless. Every task takes its own time and must mature. Persistence and patience are more important than speed, but enjoying the journey and learning something new is also important. ⦂⦂

I have the most difficulty accepting inefficiency. Whatever I do, I want to do it efficiently, whether it's work, sleep, leisure, relaxation, sports, fun, or something else. ⋮ There are two types of people in the world: those with reasons and those with results. Until we bring them into reality, even the best ideas are nothing more than daydreaming. ⋮ If we are efficient, we can change our environment and reality, influence the course of events, and make something happen. This is one of the basic needs that the human brain seems naturally equipped with. ⋮ Greater efficiency begins with clear goals. The goal must be clearly and precisely described, measurable, achievable, realistic, and time-bound. The brain works best when we set a time- and space-specific goal. Then the person can focus all their power on it and often achieve it. ⋮ A great example is writing this book. When I realized that the five years I had given myself to write the book was almost over, my mind shifted into high gear, and I managed to finish it. My goal was to give the book to Iza for her eighteenth birthday and to Živa for her twentieth birthday. ⋮ A daily routine is essential for creativity. Discipline tames our moody moods, turns all unnecessary action into automation, and allows our brains to focus only on the most important thing—the goal. And I succeeded. ⋮ So why are people unsuccessful? Because they don't take action. They think about it, dream about it, and talk about it—they talk about it a lot— but they never actually start. They don't take action. Why not? Because of the settings of the subconscious mind. ⸫

Growing up, I was taught that humility and modesty are noble virtues. However, I felt differently about these qualities in my younger years. It seemed that these virtues didn't take you very far and that society values other things more. During these searching years, putting things in the proper perspective is harder. ⋮ Nowadays, humility is a quality that's rarely attributed with much significance. The trend is to be someone. But for many people, humility has a hint of contradiction. It reminds us of humiliation, enslavement, and self-destruction. This kind of behavior creates false modesty and an imitation of humility. A truly humble person doesn't even know they're humble. ⋮ Being humble doesn't mean hiding our talents and feeling inferior or smaller than we are, but rather having a clear picture of our flaws and not feeling superior because of our strengths. Humility is a quality of great people. ⋮ True humility is based on inner strength and the realization that we neither underestimate nor overestimate ourselves but instead know our limits. It doesn't mean bowing down to someone else but bending down for someone. True humility doesn't manifest itself with modesty and humble words. ⋮ Modesty is often wrongly perceived as a sign of weakness when in reality, it's a sign of great inner strength. Modest people place great importance on actions that can help others without getting caught up in external achievements. ⋮ Over time, I realized that my parents were right and that humility and modesty are essential virtues. They're very rare and valuable. ⁞

Years ago, when I was forty-two, I took my mother to a homeopath because of her foot problems. At one point, the homeopath shifted his attention to me and asked why I smoked. I was a bit surprised. I was there for my mother, not myself. He should focus on her, I thought. But then he asked the same question again. I answered that smoking relaxed and comforted me and that I enjoyed it. And, yes, I knew it was harmful to my health and that I would eventually have to die from something. Soon, my mother joined the questioning, and just to get her to stop focusing on me, I bought some balls that were supposed to help me make the wise decision. When I got home, I threw them in a drawer and smoked happily. ⦂ One day, when I ran out of cigarettes, I remembered the little homeopathic pills and decided to try them for fun. I ate them for sixteen days and stopped smoking without any difficulty. I did not gain weight, I was not nervous (I have witnesses!), and

the cigarette smoke did not bother me. It was an exciting experience. ⦂ Giving up habits before external pressure or health issues force us to is smart. It is also an excellent way to enhance our self-esteem, which positively affects other areas of our lives. ⦂⦂

Change in society doesn't come from the outside; it starts with individuals. Our emotions are the compass nature has given us. When we are in harmony with ourselves, we act from feelings of love, compassion, trust, and joy. ⦂ At some point in life, every person is faced with the question of what's next. They question the meaning of life, happiness, success, and change. Learned helplessness and comfort zones can make us feel trapped, weak, and powerless, unable to take control of our lives. ⦂ Many people resign themselves to fate, believing that their destiny is shaped by others and that they can't do much to improve

their lives. This false belief is often unconsciously instilled by our parents, relatives, and teachers during our youth. We find more energy, time, and freedom when we accept what can't be changed and focus clearly on what can be. ⦂ To change, we must first believe that we are capable. We always have the option to change what we don't like today. Our task is to live our lives to the fullest. We can only do this by breaking out of learned patterns and limitations. ⦂ Our responsibility is to decide what beliefs and guidelines we want to live by. Our responsibility is to understand what is truly ours. We have free will—if we want to change something, it's our job to change it. Until we change our own behavior, our lives won't change. ⦂ Significant changes require bravery and a willingness to take risks. But we also risk not taking that step. Often, we risk even more. What changes us isn't what we've read but what we've experienced. ⦂ Why do we fear change? It's because we're afraid. We fear the unknown. What we know is safe, but what's different from what we know can be dangerous. We, consciously or subconsciously, see change as something negative. Even when we suffer, we persist on the path that led us to this state. We fear change, even if it's for the better. The less safe we feel, the harder it is to change. ⁝ We also resist change because it's a demanding and serious process that brings a certain level of stress, causing discomfort. Change is responsibility. People consciously and unconsciously resist change. The easiest thing is to repeat old patterns. Most people think they'll regret foolish action more than foolish inaction. ⁝ I used to be afraid of change, but now I welcome it more and more. ⁝⁝

Once upon a time, I fought an unrelenting battle against a persistent weed known as the ground elder. It was no ordinary weed, but a tenacious adversary that seemed impossible to eradicate. Despite my best efforts, I failed to uproot its long and sprawling roots. My next attempt was to douse its leaves with a potent poison, which proved fruitless. So, I called in the professionals—gardeners. They came, removed all the soil, weed, and other plants, brought in new soil, planted new plants, and left. But the ground elder didn't. I didn't have to wait long before it peeked out of the freshly tilled earth. I was at my wits' end, but I kept searching. During my research, I stumbled upon a book called *Wild Thing*, by Dario Cortese, and discovered that the ground elder is one of the most useful, healthy, and incredible plants. It's three to four times richer in minerals and vitamins than the vegetables growing around it! It combined both culinary and aromatic properties. I was thoroughly enchanted and grateful that the ground elder had defied my attempts to destroy it. From that day on, I proudly included

it in my salads. ⁝ This story is actually about reframing. I learned this technique in a course on neuro-linguistic programming and was immediately captivated by it. It seemed almost magical, and I felt like I was finally on my way to becoming my childhood hero, Pippi Longstocking. ⁝ When we can't change our thoughts or events, we can help ourselves by looking at them in a new context and thus changing our frame of mind. We can reframe every negative thought into a more positive one, every problem into a challenge, an opportunity for growth. We can deliberately choose to see a situation from a new perspective and recognize the positive aspects of the situation in which we find ourselves. ⋮ An excellent example of reframing is Mark Twain's story of Tom Sawyer, who was assigned to whitewash a fence as a punishment. He was afraid of ridicule from his peers, but he turned the task into a fun experience and even made money by selling the privilege of painting the fence to his friends. ⋮ Tom was able to reframe the chore into a sought-after pleasure, and everyone around him accepted this as reality. ⋮ Reframing has the power to influence both our reasoning and emotions. Our emotions drive us in life and make us do what we do. ⁞

The beauty of synchronicity is in its ubiquitous presence in nature; it's common in flocks of birds, schools of fish, and other forms of wildlife. Despite having hundreds of birds in one flock, they still manage to move in harmony with each other without the presence of a clear leader. These birds change their direction at the exact same moment and journey in unison, flawlessly. ⦂ Our furry friends know when we're coming home; they can sense it even before we've thought about it. Synchronicity only occurs when we have a close connection with other beings, whether human, animal, or object. Our bodies are constantly in sync; the slightest disturbance in one part of our physical body will be immediately reflected in the whole. ⦂ Wherever we go, we radiate signals on an intimate level that communicate who we are. Synchronicity is never accidental; it has a purpose and testament to our authenticity and true motives. ⁚⁚

Writing this book gives me a sense of purpose, filling me with joy. Writing is a therapeutic outlet for me and (hopefully) for those who read it. ⠇ In life, we need a mission because it gives us a sense of contributing to society's well-being. Pursuing a personal mission also develops a passion that helps us achieve our goals and overcome seemingly insurmountable obstacles. ⠇ We learn throughout our lives, mainly so we can work, because working makes us feel useful and needed. Feeling useful and needed is an indispensable feeling. When we feel useful, we feel accepted. ⠇ Feeling useless is the worst thing for a person. If we are useless, it means nobody needs us; if nobody needs us, nobody will miss us, and if nobody misses us, nobody loves us. That is why learning to be useful, practical, and desirable is essential. People are happiest when they do something from the heart, with passion and joy. ⠇ This thought reminds me of the wisdom in the Slovenian folktale »Wheat, the Prettiest Flower.« In the story, a king orders all the old people to be killed because they are no longer useful to the kingdom. When the king was looking for a husband for his daughter, he presented three challenges to the young men in the kingdom. Only one young man was successful in completing all three challenges. He had hidden his father, who helped him with answers and was the only one who proved wise. When the young man admitted to the king where his wisdom came from, the king realized that the experience and knowledge of the old people were necessary. He ordered everyone to treat the old people respectfully from that day on. ⠇ All people are worthy and equal. Everyone is unique, and the world needs precisely what that individual can and must contribute to improve the world. ⠿

12

This chapter wouldn't exist if my mother didn't slap me when I was younger. It was the only time I've ever been hit. (I hope child services doesn't find out and call my mom in for questioning.) Of course, the slap was justified. ⁝ I was doing my math homework and couldn't get it right. Then comes that familiar frustration—»I can't, I don't know, I don't understand«—with all my might, persistently … so much so that even my mom, known for her steel nerves, snapped and slapped me. I was utterly shocked and breathless. I sulked for a while, then effortlessly, without help, solved all the tasks. It reminds me of moments when a computer freezes and you have to forcefully shut it down to restart it. ⁝ When something isn't working out, we often use these lies: ⁝ »I can't help it; I've always been this way.« ⁝ »This is my nature; I inherited it and can't change it.« ⁝ »My family is responsible for my personality.« ⁝ »I am a prisoner of culture and time.« ⁝ Whenever we say, »I can't,« in life, what we really mean is, »I won't,« or, »I don't want to.« When we say, »I can't,« we often behave like victims—helpless before our challenges. ⁝ Let's replace »I can't« with something more honest, like »I don't want to.« »Hard« doesn't mean »impossible.« When we focus on something, this focus immediately creates ideas and thought patterns we wouldn't have otherwise. In fact, we can influence the physical world and all our circumstances by how we use our thoughts. ⁝ *»It's not what you are that holds you back; it's what you think you're not.«* Denis Waitley ⁝⁝

Our thoughts are important. Very important. At the beginning of this book, I compared life to a car. And when you're driving, navigation is of immense help. With navigation, we choose the paths that lead us to our destination. It's the same with our thoughts. They help us determine the course that will take us to our desired goal. Sometimes we choose the quickest route, sometimes the shortest, and sometimes we deviate from the ideal path to discover something new. ⦂ However, today people have a better grasp of navigation

devices than their thoughts. Many people are unaware that their thoughts can be changed and that they can influence the future. ⦂ Our thoughts have such powerful consequences that they can create our reality. We can't directly choose our circumstances, but we can choose our thoughts and, in turn, shape our circumstances. Our thoughts attract certain situations and people into our lives, so our thoughts must be positive to attract positive people and events. ⦂ Our thoughts don't just create our future; they can also hold us back in the past and make our lives difficult. It's normal for our thoughts to wander into the past or future occasionally, but it becomes dangerous when we dwell there too long. It's essential to let go of the past and move on. It may not always be easy, but it's necessary. ⦂ Navigation must remain in our hands, so we can create the life that we want and remain the masters of our own happiness. ⠿

THE IMPACT OF
HABITS ON YOUR LIFE

I've always struggled with getting out of bed in the morning. It was a long and drawn-out process, and the snooze button was my closest companion. But it wasn't a friend to my brain, as I later learned from some scientific studies that hitting the snooze button is the worst thing you can do. Because our brain is no joke and our body loves routine and predictability, I decided to change this habit and bid farewell to the snooze button. ⠇

I tackled this by moving my phone alarm from the bedroom to the bathroom, and it worked. When it rings, I have no choice but to get up and turn it off. ⠇

I then took on another challenge. I had heard constantly about the benefits of waking up early, how it's healthy and positively impacts our lives and inner balance. Our body has an internal clock; we need to listen to it to have more energy and incredible zest for life. The processes and stages that provide our body optimal efficiency and function are carefully scheduled hour by hour, and we should not interrupt or disrupt them. ⁝ I started by moving my wake-up time from 7:00 a.m. to 6:00 a.m. and two years later, from 6:00 a.m. to 5:00 a.m. I decided that the fateful day I would start waking up at 5:00 a.m. would be March 1, 2020. It was crazy that it was a Sunday—and even crazier that it was raining. In short, I would have spent most of the day in bed, warm and cozy, in the old days. But I didn't. I do what I say. ⁝ Habits can be a blessing or a curse. Almost everything we do is determined by our habits. Once a habit is formed, it can't be undone. We can only replace it with a newer, better version. We shape our habits, and then they shape us. Good habits are hard to develop but easy to live with, while bad habits are easy to develop but hard to live with. ⁝ People only change their habits if they are forced to. We must change the underlying motives to change behavior, which means changing the entire pattern. The energy to change the pattern comes when our old practice no longer works. ⁝ Our habits aren't our fate. We can ignore, change, or replace them. Habits are powerful but vulnerable. They can form without our awareness but can also be consciously planned. Often, they form without our permission, but we can shape them if we focus on their components. They impact our lives more than we think—that's how strong they are because our brains cling to them more than anything else, including sound reason. ⁝ The most important habit is strong willpower. The best way to build will is to turn self-discipline into a routine. Sometimes people aren't making much effort with self-control—but that's because they've made it automatic. Their willpower works without them having to think about it. ⁝ We can't erase old habits; we can only change them. Everything we do is either for ourselves or against ourselves. Everything in life is a choice. ⁝⁝

A young girl had two apples. »Can you please give me one?« her mother asked. The little girl quickly took a bite out of one apple, then immediately took another bite out of the other. ⁝ Her mother looked at her daughter with disappointment and sadness. But the daughter handed her one of the apples and said, »Here you go, Mom. This one is sweeter!« ⁝ Don't Judge! Because you don't know … ⁝ Every time we judge others, we must remember that what we judge them for is within us too. What we see in others is actually a reflection of ourselves. This can be uncomfortable, but it's also a learning

opportunity. It's a chance to better understand ourselves and realize what lies within us. We can only recognize in others what is within us. ⁝⁝

Overgeneralization can be dangerous because it often creates stereotypes and a distorted view of people and situations around us. Things are never *all* good or *all* bad. Not *everyone* thinks the same way. You haven't lost *everything*. You don't know *nothing*. Not *everything* goes wrong for you. You don't *always* arrive late. These types of statements and thinking are shallow and meaningless. We resort to overgeneralization when we don't take the time to delve deeper or gather the correct information, when we're too lazy to think or don't care to. ⋮ Take charge of your thoughts and perceptions, avoid overgeneralizing, and see the world with a more precise, confident, and independent mindset. Make informed decisions and trust your abilities to navigate the world in a productive, autonomous, and assertive manner. ⁚⁚

»It is not the critic who counts; not the man who points out how the strong man stumbles, or where the doer of deeds could have done them better. The credit belongs to the man who is actually in the arena, whose face is marred by dust and sweat and blood; who strives valiantly; who errs, who comes short again and again, because there is no effort without error and short-coming; but who does actually strive to do the deeds; who knows great enthusiasms, the great devotions; who spends himself in a worthy cause; who at the best knows in the end the triumph of high achievement, and who at the worst, if he fails, at least fails while daring greatly, so that his place shall never be with those cold and timid souls who neither know victory nor defeat.« *Theodore Roosevelt*

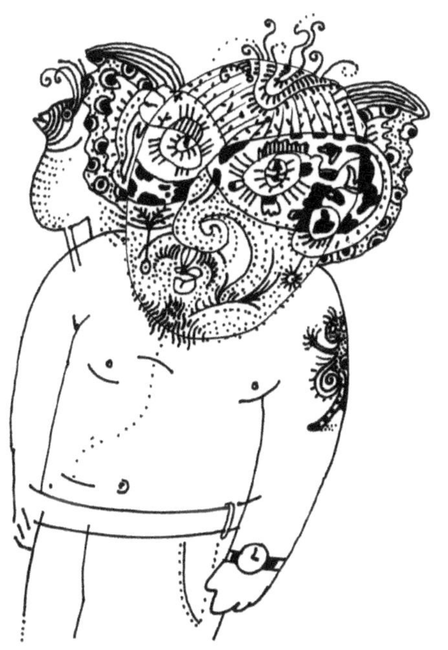

Years ago, Dragan and I vacationed in Barbados. The hotel was great, but it was inundated with warnings. We were warned about every potential danger—slippery floors, stairs, the depth of the pool … ⫶ Every day we played tennis, and there were even more warnings there that we were playing at our own risk. One day, shortly after a rain shower, we went to the tennis court, which was still slightly wet on the sides. The court was concrete, so we quickly brushed off the few puddles. The hotel manager rushed to the court and tried to save us from certain death. At least, that's what it looked like. She was frightened and warned us that the wet surface was dangerous and that we could get hurt. After a lengthy discussion, she called a »specialist« to assess the »danger« level. She seemed relieved when she could pass on the responsibility for any possible accident to someone else. It was a very nice young man who we saw daily on the beach, mowing the grass and maintaining cleanliness. He was a simple guy who had a lot of common sense. I'll always remember his words: »Things in life are very simple until  people complicate them. Enjoy the game.« ⫶ *»It's a simple matter to make things complex, but a complex matter to make things simple.«* ⫶ Meyer's Law ⫶ Why do we do foolish things? ⫶ I came up with three reasons. The first is that we genuinely lack common sense, the second is that we're frightened, and the third is that we have common sense but make foolish decisions to benefit ourselves. ⫶⫶

An obituary printed in the London Times. ⁞ Today we mourn the passing of a beloved old friend, »Common Sense,« who has been with us for many years. ⁞ No one knows for sure how old he was, since his birth records were long ago lost in bureaucratic red tape and political correctness. He will be remembered as having cultivated such valuable lessons as: Knowing when to come in out of the rain; why the early bird gets the worm; Life isn't always fair; and maybe it was my fault. ⁞ Common Sense lived by simple, sound financial policies (don't spend more than you can earn) and reliable strategies (adults, not children, are in charge). His health began to deteriorate rapidly when well-intentioned but overbearing regulations were set in place. Reports of a 6-year-old boy charged with sexual harassment for kissing a classmate; teens suspended from school for using mouthwash after lunch; and a teacher fired for reprimanding an unruly student, only worsened his condition. ⁞ Common Sense lost ground when parents attacked teachers for doing the job that they themselves had failed to do in disciplining their unruly children. It declined even further when schools were required to get parental consent to administer sun lotion or an aspirin to a student; but could not inform parents when a student became pregnant and wanted to have an abortion. ⁞ Common Sense lost the will to live as the churches became businesses; and criminals received better treatment than their victims. Common Sense took a beating when you couldn't defend yourself from a burglar in your own home and the burglar could sue you for assault. Common Sense finally gave up the will to live, after a woman failed to realise that a steaming cup of coffee was hot. She spilled a little in her lap, and was promptly awarded a huge settlement ... Common Sense was preceded in death, by his parents, Truth and Trust. His wife, Discretion, his daughter, Responsibility, his son, Reason,

He is survived by his 4 stepbrothers; I Know My Rights; I want it now; Someone Else Is To Blame; I'm A Victim. Not many attended his funeral because so few realised he was gone. If you still remember him, pass this on. If not, join the majority and do nothing ...

THE TRUE VALUE
OF LUXURY

Luxury is living life under desired conditions. I don't embrace material-
ism, but I do love aesthetics. To me, less is more, so I carefully choose even
the most minor things. Quality isn't elitism to me; it's sustainability. ⦚ The
things that have brought me the most joy in life and what I was willing to
pay the most for are those that have contributed to my independence and
freedom. ⦚⦚

UNCOVERING THE TRUE MEANING
OF HAPPINESS

Happiness is mainly dependent on the state of our minds. While external
circumstances can play a role, the key to happiness is to have good health,
live a fulfilling life, think effectively, do work we enjoy, and have wisdom.
Good relationships—both personal and professional—can also contribute
significantly to overall happiness. ⦚ If our happiness relies on changes
made by others, we will never be truly happy, constantly feeling the need
for others to change. Happiness is an emotion, like joy, sadness, hate, guilt,
jealousy, and others. It has causes that we can understand and control. Happiness is multi-faceted and can be defined in many ways. Sometimes we
need to work for it; other times, it comes naturally. Regardless of how we
define happiness, we all strive for it. ⦚ We are happy when we care about
something greater than ourselves. We are happy when we believe we are
a part of something greater. We are happy when we feel useful. ⦚ The for-
giveness of others is essential for mental peace and excellent health. If we

want complete health and happiness, we must forgive everyone who has hurt us. If we love ourselves, we take care not to live with grudges. ⋮ For me, happiness is the freedom to live life as I want, to be loved, and to have someone to love. I am happy when I make others happy. Good deeds return to me as a feeling of happiness and give me energy. I am happy. ⁞

In his book *The Subtle Art of Not Giving a F*ck*, author Mark Manson argues that the beauty of poker lies in the fact that luck is always a factor, but it does not dictate the long-term outcome. You can be dealt terrible cards and still beat someone who has been dealt great cards. Of course, the person with the better cards is more likely to win, but the ultimate winner is determined by the decisions made during the game. ⦂ I similarly see life. We all are dealt different cards—some better, some worse. And while it's easy to become self-conscious about bad cards and feel like life has dealt us a poor hand, it's the decisions we make with those cards, the risks we're willing to take, and the consequences we're willing to live with that represent the real game. Those who consistently make the best decisions in given situations are the ones who ultimately win at poker, just as in life. And they're not necessarily the ones with the best cards. ⦂ I'm grateful to accept life as it comes and don't feel the need to force my ideas onto it. Its ideas are much better than mine, especially since it can see farther and wider than I can and knows what's best to happen or not. It's a fantastic feeling to surrender to it, a sense of freedom. ⦂ I've realized that we're all masters, as we can create different endings to the chapters of our lives. Every day is my birthday. Every day I'm born again. New. Different. Better. ⦂

Meeting someone after a long time can make them seem to have aged quite a bit. Of course, we never see ourselves as »aged.« Nevertheless, time leaves its mark on each and every one of us. In the past, I was fifty-five years old when a salesperson in a children's clothing store asked me if I was buying a gift for my granddaughter. I was like, »Hell no, I still feel thirty-five.« It was quite a shock and not a small one. ⁝ At what age does a person feel old? What makes us feel old? The first gray hair, back pain, or something else? It depends on how we view aging. If we haven't achieved what we or those around us deem necessary at a certain age, we may feel old even in our prime years. ⁝ When we're young, we often pretend to be older. We want people to take us seriously. We want the privileges that come with being older. This is especially true in the business world. We dress and act like our more senior colleagues to earn the trust of business partners. Of course, this depends on the environment in which we operate. Sometimes youth and craziness are valued more than maturity and wisdom. ⁝ Aging is the ultimate test of beauty. External youthful charm transforms into inner beauty that radiates outward and becomes nobler with time. Being beautiful means being pleasing to the eye, regardless of age. Style is obtained through moderation and taste. Style is not only displayed in the contours and physical presence but is also a sign of intelligence, which comes from within. It's a choice, a perception of ourselves, what we are, what we want to become, and how we want to achieve it. Taking care of ourselves and having a pleasant appearance is not a vain act but a matter of respect. ⁝ A person can be young or old at any age. But they are always young enough to enjoy life to the fullest! There's always something new to learn. And experience is our best teacher. Youth rarely understands many things that become self-evident in old age. That's why I love the aging process. Through many life experiences, our inner strength must be revealed in all its glory. ⋮ I see myself as a constantly evolving being, and I wouldn't go back to the past for anything. Aging is a beautiful thing. No wrinkles are worth giving up on the experiences I've gained over the years. ⋮ It's essential to keep a youthful spirit and an open mind, to continue learning, to have fun, and to never lose the spark of mischief. Trust me, it pays off. ⋮ People on their deathbeds rarely regret not controlling their lives enough. They regret not taking more risks, not following their dreams, and letting their passions die. Most of all, they regret not opening their hearts, not expressing their love, and not letting go of the armor they wore to protect themselves. ⋮⋮

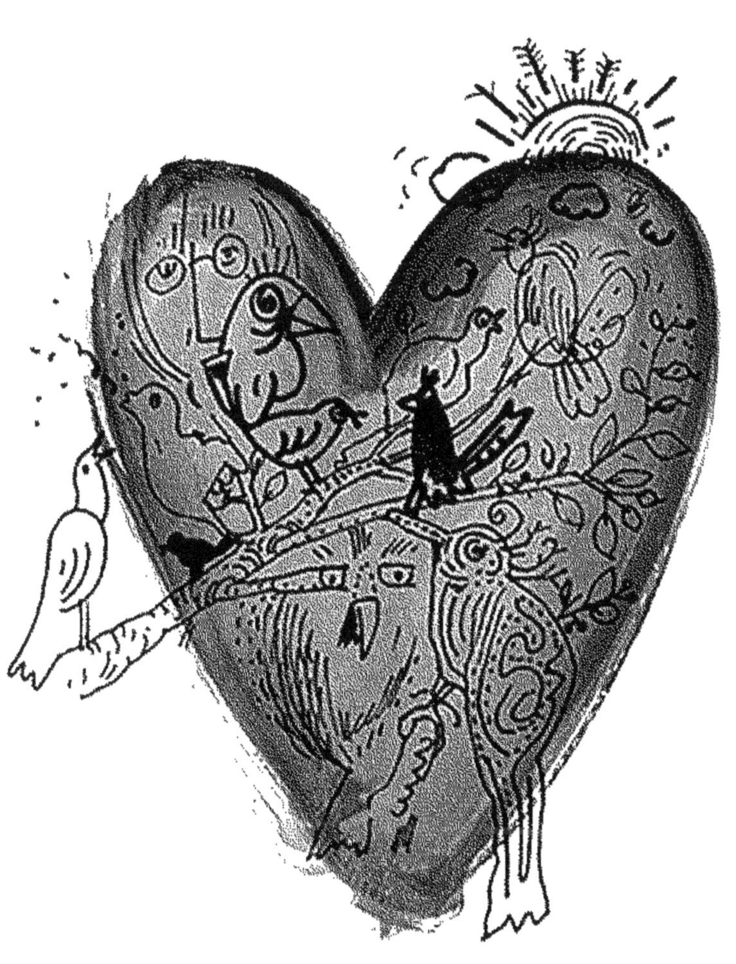

Aunt Justa could be described with one word: activist. She never married or had her own children, but she cared for many others, not just her relatives. ⋮ People can be divided into those who seek problems and those who seek solutions. Aunt Justa belonged to the latter group. She never hesitated to lend a helping hand, bring or organize something. She did everything with ease. ⋮ I must admit, I didn't visit her during the last days of her life. I couldn't, not because of a lack of time, but because I couldn't bear it. I wanted to keep her in my memory as she was, healthy and in excellent shape. ⋮ Whenever I spoke to my mother, I asked her how Aunt Justa was doing. I confided in her that I couldn't visit. My mother understood. She saw Aunt Justa every week. When I asked my mother how she could do it, she replied, »Once I heard about someone seriously ill and lying in the hospital. He said that the power to heal came from those who visited him.« From that moment on, I never even thought that I couldn't. ⋮ The death of a loved one can be accepted as a catastrophe, or we can realize how lucky we were to have that person in our lives. ⦂⦂

Time is arguably the most elusive of all human experiences. We can't catch it or take a picture of it. We can't store it in one place to use later elsewhere. The only way we can describe time is through the events within it: ⋮ An old man is cutting wood in the forest. A traveler asks, »Excuse me, how long does it take to get to the city?« And the old man keeps cutting, looks at him, and then returns to cutting. The traveler touches his shoulder and asks again, »Excuse me, how long does it take to get to the city, please?« The old man keeps cutting, looks at him, and returns to cutting. ⋮ The traveler thinks to himself, »Well, that's that.« ⋮ He goes on his way, and the moment he leaves, the old man stops cutting the wood, turns around, looks after him, and calls out, »Ten minutes!« ⋮ The traveler returns to the old man and says, »Excuse me, but I asked you twice and you couldn't answer. Then I go away and you yell after me. Are you trying to irritate me?« ⋮ And the old man replies, »How? I had to first see how fast you walked!« ⋮ This old man's approach to time reminds us that it's not just about the numbers but also about the experience and the journey. Time is a personal experience, and it's up to us to make the most of it. Be confident, empowered, and decisive in your time use. Trust yourself and be autonomous, efficient, and productive in every moment. ⋮ *»Time is too slow for those who wait, too swift for those who fear, too long for those who grieve, too short for those who rejoice, but for those who love, time is eternity.«* Henry Van Dyke ⫶

The past is always with us. The inability or unpreparedness of the human mind to leave the past behind is beautifully depicted in the story of two Zen monks: ⋮ The Zen monks were returning to the monastery. When they reached the river, they encountered a young girl kneeling on the bank and crying. ⋮ »What's wrong?« asked the older monk. ⋮ »My mother is dying. She's in the house on the other side of the river, but I can't cross it. I tried,« the girl continued, »but the current grabbed me. I'll never be able to make it to the other side without help … I thought I would never see my mother alive again. But now … now that you're here, maybe you can help me cross the river.« ⋮ »I wish we could,« the younger one said regretfully. »But we can only help you by carrying you across, and our vow of chastity prevents us from having physical contact with the opposite sex.« ⋮ »I'm sorry too,« the girl replied, and cried again. ⋮ The older monk knelt down, bowed his head, and said to her, »Climb onto my back.« ⋮ The woman couldn't believe it, but she quickly took her cane and climbed onto the monk's back. He struggled to cross the river with the burden, followed by the younger monk. When they reached the other side, the woman wanted to kiss the monk's hand as a sign of gratitude. ⋮ »It's okay, it's okay,« the elder said, withdrawing his hand. »Just go.« The woman gratefully bowed and took her things, running down the path toward the village. ⋮ The monks continued their walk in silence. They had ten more hours of walking ahead of them. Just before they arrived at their destination, the younger monk said to the elder, »Master, you know the vow of chastity better than I do, but you still carried that woman across the wide river.« ⋮ »Yes, I carried her across the river, but I also put her down. What's wrong with you? Why are you still carrying her?« ⁞ The past lives within us as memories, but memories themselves don't cause problems. Memories allow us to learn from the past and past mistakes. Only when memories and thoughts about the past possess us entirely do they become a burden, a problematic and integral part of our current sense of self. ⁞⁞

THE PRESENT

It takes great courage to surrender to the present moment, but it's the only way to create a better future. The only thing we truly have control over is right now, the moment that shapes our future. »Live life one day at a time.« It's more challenging than it sounds. ⁞⁞

THE FUTURE

Our future is flexible. We have the power to shape it simply by observing its potential possibilities. ⁞ I've come to realize that my expectations have an impact on what will happen. In a way, I create my own reality. Whenever I approach something with negative biases, the outcomes are also adverse. That's why I'm mindful of my thoughts. I believe that energy follows thoughts, and thoughts come before actions. This means that I can influence my life and that everything around me is merely a reflection of it. In reality, the inner world creates the outer world. ⁞⁞

BECOMING REAL

A remarkable story about how to become real is described in the book *The Velveteen Rabbit* by Margery Williams. ⁞ In the story, two children's toys, the Skin Horse and the Velveteen Rabbit, discuss how toys become real: ⁞

»What is REAL?« asked the Rabbit one day when they were lying side by side near the nursery fender before Nana came to tidy the room. »Does it mean having things that buzz inside you and a stick-out handle?« ⁝ »Real isn't how you are made,« said the Skin Horse. »It's a thing that happens to you. When a child loves you for a long, long time, not just to play with, but REALLY loves you, then you become Real.« ⁝ »Does it hurt?« asked the Rabbit. ⁝ »Sometimes,« said the Skin Horse, for he was always truthful. »When you are Real you don't mind being hurt.« ⁝ »Does it happen all at once, like being wound up,« he asked, »or bit by bit?« ⁝ »It doesn't happen all at once,« said the Skin Horse. »You become. It takes a long time. That's why it doesn't often happen to people who break easily, or have sharp edges, or who have to be carefully kept. Generally, by the time you are Real, most of your hair has been loved off and your eyes drop out and you get loose in the joints and very shabby. But these things don't matter at all, because once you are Real you can't be ugly, except to people who don't understand.« ⁝ »I suppose you are Real?« said the Rabbit. And then he wished he had not said it, for he thought the Skin Horse might be sensitive. But the Skin Horse only smiled. ⁝ »The Boy's Uncle made me Real,« he said. »That was a great many years ago; but once you are Real you can't become unreal again. It lasts for always.«

During my teenage years, I had to care for my sister, Simona, who has developmental disorders. It's not an easy task for a teenager already facing many »big« problems. ⦙ One day, the day of my final exams, my sister decided she wasn't attending school. She was yelling, hitting, and resisting in every possible way. My task was to escort her to the school bus. Of course, we missed it, and I desperately offered to drive her to school in my dad's car. It was the only option if I didn't want to miss my final exams, so we went. But first, we ran into a little problem. When exiting the garage, I wasn't paying attention, and boom! There was a dent in the middle of the hood. I took Simona to school anyway and went to my final exams all frazzled. What would Dad say? ⦙ Did a confrontation with my dad follow? Of course not. Instead of dealing with the problem right away, I waited for my dad to notice the damage to the car. He was commuting to work by bike, which meant my torment lasted a while before the day of the confrontation arrived. Trembling with fear, I watched through the window as my dad drove out of the garage and spotted the dent. I didn't know how to deal with my fears then. ⦙ My dad was not happy, to say the least. He was even less happy when I told him it happened on the day of my final exams. He just said he hoped I passed. ⦙ I offered to earn money for the repair through summer work and pay him back for the damage. He declined. Well, in the end, it wasn't so

bad after all. Living in fear was by far the most challenging part. ⫶ Fear is the most significant danger we face on the path of growing up. Fear is like an epidemic in today's society. We're afraid of beginnings and what will happen in the end. We're scared of change or getting stuck. We're afraid of success and failure alike. We're scared of life and death too. ⫶ Fear forces us to cling to old habits and limits our flexibility. Behind our adult masks, we still hide a frightened child who is afraid of not being accepted for who they are. Our inner child is often terrified and unconsciously reacts to things that happened in our childhood. But our response to social influences shakes in adulthood, and all the ways we try to protect our self-image, limiting beliefs, interpersonal relationships, safety, and view of the world, are also developing. Unhealed traumas from the past trigger fears in the present, and our inner child wants to ensure we protect what's essential to it. ⫶ We let ourselves be led by fears because we don't know how to do it any other way. When we start looking at loss as an opportunity for growth and a new beginning, we stop being afraid, start accepting what is, and absorb the lessons that life is trying to teach us. Courage is not about fearlessness, but about allowing fear to reshape us so we can achieve the right attitude toward uncertainty, peace with instability, and awareness of who we are. ⫶ When we realize that nothing in life is random, that we were not victims of misfortune, bad genes, or hostile forces, and that even illnesses and people who hurt us were teachers of our soul deserving gratitude—only then are we ready to change our attitude toward fear and uncertainty. We taught everyone how to behave toward us. Peace comes when we simply accept everything that happens. ⫶ There's nothing in life to be afraid of. It just needs to be understood. The more you understand, the less you fear. ⁝⁝

For a few years now, I have been without a television, I don't listen to news reports, and I only follow the media enough to know what the world is currently dealing with and to understand why people act the way they do, to find out which »facts« might influence their thoughts and actions. ⋮ Why? Because I don't know what is true and what isn't from what is written and heard. When I read a news article about an event I was very familiar with because I was involved in it, I realized that not even »serious« media can be fully trusted. Some news articles are lacking, and some misleading or incorrect. The reason may be that the reporter only superficially knows the issue because of a lack of time, resources, superficiality, or all of the above. The reason could also be because of his/her »flexible« spine, allowing him/her to report on an event as instructed. ⋮ I don't spend time guessing what is true and 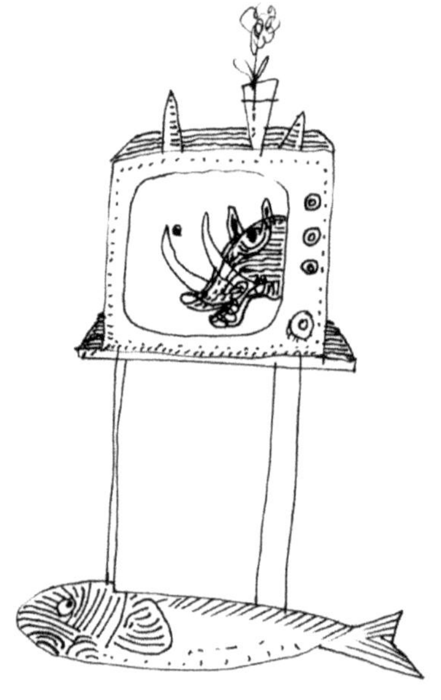 what isn't, creating opinions based on insufficient, false, or fabricated news. I still happily follow journalists who do their work with heart and honesty. ⋮ An excessive amount of information steals our time, and it is becoming increasingly difficult to isolate oneself. Some of us who have had enough of this and want to take a break would like to retreat from this madness and focus on ourselves. Absence is becoming comfort: lack of sounds, information, and images. ⁝

You may not fully understand this chapter at your current age of eighteen or twenty, but it will be grasped by anyone who happens to come across this guide and is over … years of age. It's not that you won't know how to use various electronic devices and gadgets in your older years. (I wrote this book on my iPhone, iPad, and Mac.) The issue is that we view these devices from above, and the reflection on the screen reveals wrinkles that were previously unknown to us. It's quite a shock for someone who feels youthful and energetic to see an aging, lost lady staring back at them from the screen's reflection. ⦂ I haven't yet experienced a harsher moment of truth about my physical appearance than this one. It just has to reveal itself to you. ⦂⦂

Our society is obsessed with unrealistic and unattainable expectations. The constant barrage of messages to be happier, healthier, and more successful has created a generation that believes it's not okay to experience negative emotions. Social media feeds are filled with carefully curated posts of people having a blast while you're sitting at home, feeling like your life is pathetic. No wonder we often feel like there's something wrong with us. ⁝ The more we strive for something, the less satisfied we become. The relentless pursuit of wealth, status, or material possessions only serves to reinforce the fact that we don't have what we want. It's a vicious cycle that leaves us feeling empty and unfulfilled. ⁝ But there's a better way. We can choose to live life on our own terms, independent and autonomous. When we prioritize our goals and desires, we become empowered to create a life that truly makes us happy. We can find true satisfaction and fulfillment by embracing our individuality and pursuing our own path. ⁘

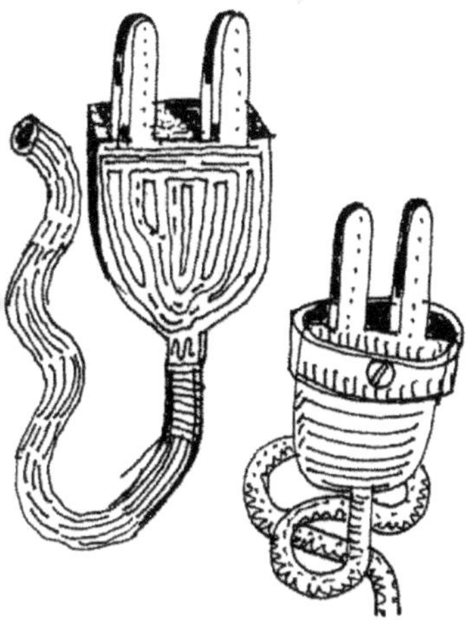

Unfortunately, the world is headed strangely, where Uncle Google increasingly controls people's lives. Google offers people more and more content about things they've shown interest in. ⁝ For example: ⁝ People interested in healthy eating will suddenly be bombarded with ads and content about how to look and feel healthy for a long time. ⁝ A person who is afraid they've fallen ill and is browsing pages with various diagnoses will receive even more content on this topic and suddenly feel like they are being threatened by the risk of infection everywhere … ⁝ People who click on positive content that confirms that we live in abundance and that there is enough for everyone will live in that reality. ⁝ And people who click on negative content will receive daily confirmations that there is not enough of anything and that they can lose everything at any time. ⁝ I think these are the parallel realities we live in. The internet creates people's realities. ⁝⁝

The Philippines. One of my most beautiful vacations. I learned a lot on this trip and did many things for the first time. For the first time, I traveled with a group, rode on the roof of a jeep, slept in a room with strangers, and swam in cold water … ⋮ I was lucky to have an excellent travel companion, Lučka. She taught me a lot. A retired English and German professor and an experienced traveler, she impressed me with her packing method. Before each trip, she goes shopping at a second-hand store, investing about twenty euros in new old clothes that she gradually gets rid of on the trip, to the delight of the locals. She washed her underwear by jumping into a river wearing it. ⋮ On such a trip, we realize how we have complicated our lives, how little we actually need to be happy and have fun. The most important thing of all is good company. Everything else is less important and can be solved. ⋮ And, yes, the more of the world we see, the more we appreciate home. ⋮⋮

For the past three years, I've been living alone for the first time. When I was twenty-five, I moved from home and started living with Dragan. I had never given myself a chance to experience living alone before, but now I realize it's a necessary part of life. I believe everyone should take some time to be alone. ⋮ I cherish solitude. I see it as a privilege, not a challenge. Solitude is a crucial ingredient for growth, reflection, and productive work. Alone time allows us to discover ourselves, new people, and things and to experience personal growth. There's so much to learn about life; time and solitude are essential for enrichment. The amount of solitude we need varies from person to person, but it's important to give it to ourselves and others. ⋮ The ability to be alone is often a sign of a strong personality. Often, people have faced tough challenges in life and come out on the other side. Some choose solitude, while others have it imposed on them. But regardless of how we get there, the ability to be alone is a valuable trait. It promotes curiosity, learning, thinking, innovation, and change and keeps us in touch with our inner imagination. Being alone makes us stronger. The happiest people are those who can balance both—intense social interactions and the enjoyment of solitude. ⋮⋮

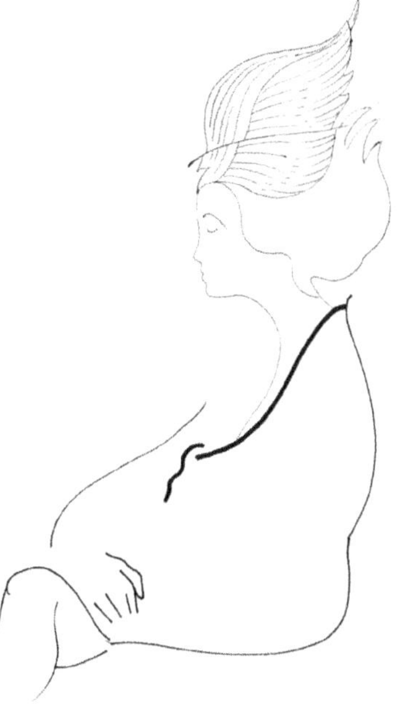

The moment can change our lives. We often read and listen to stories about it, but we don't realize the power of the moment until it touches us personally. Only then, when we find ourselves in a situation that can change our life forever, do we become aware of it. ⁝ I was driving to my mother's eighty-first birthday celebration when I overlooked an older lady due to the large crowd of Sunday walkers merging onto the main road. And then it happened. I touched her with my car, and she fell. I cannot describe that moment in words. I felt terrible. I got out of the car and helped the lady get up. Witnesses were screaming at me like I was a killer. People react differently in panic. ⁝ The lady looked okay. I drove her home so she could change before going to the emergency room. I felt it was right to call the police. While waiting for them, we chatted about this and that, about life. She mentioned that she was eighty-one years old and had severe osteoporosis, an artificial hip, a pacemaker, and some vascular clamps . . . »That's quite something,« one could say. Given all that she listed, it would have been a miracle if she didn't break something in the fall. I was apprehensive. ⁝ When the police arrived, we went to the accident scene and completed the formalities, and the lady went to the emergency

room to check for any injuries. Unfortunately, I didn't have her phone number and couldn't check on her health. I was shaking all night and slept very badly. The next day, I went to see her to check how she was feeling. Fortunately, she had no injuries, and I could finally relax. ⋮ Even though I wasn't aggressive, wasn't too hasty, wasn't on the phone, wasn't drinking, wasn't… I could have been responsible for someone's life. I overlooked her, and the lady could have died in a moment from an awkward fall, a head injury, or fear. ⋮ Everything that happens to us happens for a reason. Situations usually show us how we are being tested. When faced with a challenge, we reveal who and what we are. ⁞

The events from the previous chapter taught me several valuable lessons. When I came home after the accident, I was still shaken up. I called my neighbor and told her I needed a shoulder, whiskey, and a conversation. She said, »Yes, of course, but can it be a bit later? I'm just cleaning out my cabinet. If it's urgent, I'll come right now.« Her response took me aback, and I replied, »No, there's no need to come right now; I'll make lunch first.« When I hung up the phone, I burst into tears. Why didn't she understand that I needed her *now*? If someone says they need a shoulder, whiskey, and a conversation, they clearly mean *now*! After lunch, I gradually calmed down and decided to go to the sauna and meditate. I informed my neighbor and told her we'd meet another time. At that moment, she realized she didn't handle the situation correctly. She wanted to come right then, but I couldn't talk about it. I wanted to be alone. ⋮ We met the next day. She came with a guilty conscience and a bottle of whiskey while I was still reeling from the previous day. We talked about each other's reactions. My neighbor said she couldn't tell from my call that I was panicking. She said I sounded calm, like someone who has everything under control and can handle the situation. Someone capable. I always act like I'm capable because I try not to burden others. And I am capable. But sometimes I also need someone to offer me a shoulder, whiskey, and a conversation so that I can be capable more easily. ⋮ The lessons we learned from this experience made us think. My neighbor learned to respond immediately when she receives a call like that instead of waiting until she finishes organizing her damn files, while I learned that when I need help, I should clearly express it. If my call for help goes unnoticed, I must shout louder and more clearly.

⋮ When people react incorrectly in a given situation, it doesn't mean they're bad. They may just react clumsily, as Zlata described her actions. We learn from each other. People in our lives are our mirrors. They allow us to grow and change. ⋮ There's nothing more important than having the courage to say, »I don't know,« or, »I made a mistake.« If you make a mistake, clean it up. Being open and honest is the key to success in life. ⋮ Life lessons always come at a cost: money, health, time, friendship ... It's probably the only way to make sure we remember them. It's great if we learn the lesson the first time, but if not, education can be expensive and time-consuming. ⋮ Every time something unpleasant happens, we must recognize that it's happening for a reason, to teach us something. We must pay attention and try to understand the *why*. The answer may take time to come, but it will come eventually. ⁞⁞

During tough times, we need real friends—not just Facebook friends. During these moments, we find out who our true friends are, the ones who take the time to comfort us, embrace us, bring us tissues, cook us a healing soup, take us on a trip, or prescribe Bach Flower Remedies. ⁞ True friends may also scold us, but only if it's the only cure for our problems. It's important to listen to them and act on their advice if we find it valuable. Sometimes, we may not realize this at the moment, but we need to trust. Trusting the right friend who can offer wise counsel based on their knowledge and experience is crucial in overcoming our struggles. We can't expect one friend to solve all our problems. We need to pick someone competent enough to advise us on specific challenges. ⁞ If we want to use life's challenges positively, we must have the courage to recognize our weaknesses, shortcomings, and mistakes, accept them, and learn from them. We must be brave enough to face the pain accompanying shame, persist, and rise above it. ⁞ Life often throws us major challenges, not because it's cruel, but to offer us a final opportunity to learn to deal with ourselves.
It's just a test that we must endure if we want to find balance in life. ⁞⁞

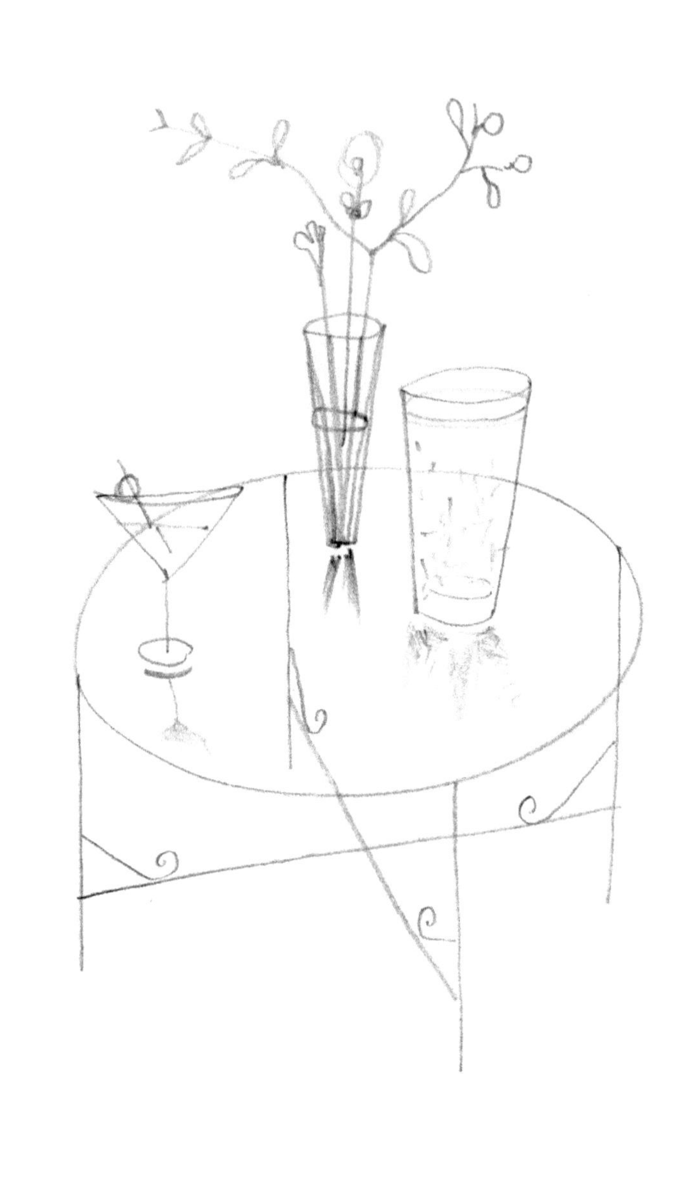

Once during a conversation with my friend Ksenija, I thought about how to cheer her up. When I asked her how she was doing, she responded with a long list of things going wrong, making her angry, or generally making her feel bad. ⋮ That's when I realized that positive thoughts and habits should multiply just as effectively as negative ones. I suggested she start doing one thing that brings her joy and puts her in a good mood. Then, as soon as possible, she should add another thought or habit, so they can keep other company and multiply. ⋮ Of course, she needs to create good conditions for them to grow and thrive. This means that every day, she should make sure that positive thoughts and habits feel great in her company, attract others to them, and slowly push out the negative ones. Eventually, the negative ones will be in the minority and need to find another host to provide better conditions for their well-being and reproduction. ⸬

Just like a plant is limited by the size of its pot and the soil quality it is planted in, humans are also placed in specific frameworks by the people accompanying us on our journey—our family, friends, teachers, and society. ⁝ But just as a plant outgrows its pot and the soil can no longer sustain it, humans also outgrow the limitations placed on them at birth. It's time to transplant yourself, choose your path, and develop the conditions to live authentically and create a fulfilling life. ⁝ If you don't take action and stay within the confines set by others, you will inevitably wither away unfulfilled and dissatisfied. Don't let yourself be limited—embrace growth and start living the life you were meant to live. ⁝⁝

Our unconscious mind is at work 24/7, storing all of our thoughts. Each of these thoughts holds the key to our potential for success. Our inner world creates our outer world. ⦂ We can learn to choose our thoughts wisely. We decide to be kind, happy, and loving, and people will reciprocate. Let's strive to keep our spirit filled with the belief that good things will happen and make sure to »control« our thoughts by directing them toward positive, beautiful, and meaningful things. ⦂ Energy follows thoughts, and thoughts precede actions. This means we are responsible for our lives, and the world around us simply reflects that. ⦂ In a sense, we are constantly creating. We can instruct our unconscious mind to choose only appropriate things in the future. ⦂ If we do what we've always done, we'll get what we've always gotten. We set our own limits. Life starts each day anew. ⦂ All of our experiences, events, circumstances, and actions are caused by our subconscious mind in response to our thoughts. Our unconscious mind is no joke. It holds us accountable. We must learn to trust our inner voice; then, things will simply be known to us. ⦂⦂

Antoine de Saint-Exupéry brought the wisdom of simple understanding of the world and uncovered some of the greatest life lessons. ⁞ Five Pieces of Wisdom from the Little Prince: ⁞ Everyone who appears in our life is important; the difference is only in the size of the seal they leave in us. Some

stay forever, and others come for just a visit. People come and go, sometimes sadly, even those we would like to keep in our lives. Every relationship with others needs to be nurtured and respected. Every friendship is unique, capturing unforgettable moments and showing how wonderful life can be. You can have one close friend, who you trust with everything, or you can have many. Thousands of people have names or surnames that are the same or similar to those of our friends. Thousands have similar appearances or heights, but only one will be the one we'll remember forever. The rare few are those for whom we're willing to do anything. Yet each one of them is unique to us. ⁞ As the Little Prince said, »It is only with the heart that one

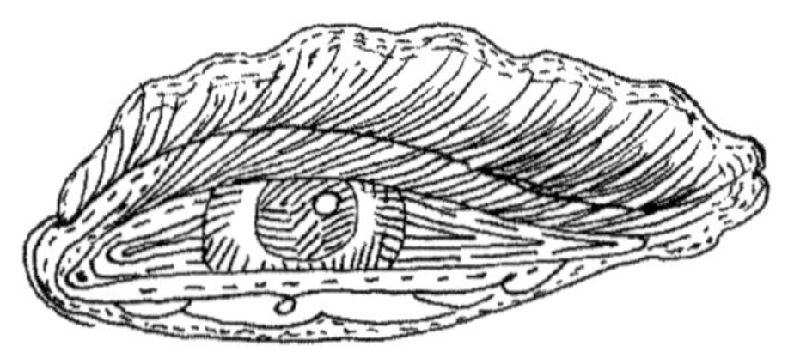

can see rightly; what is essential is invisible to the eye.« ⋮ Not even an eagle-sharp eye, understanding all theories, or knowing all the books in the world can help you if you can't see the world with your heart. A big-hearted person is a great person. One who doesn't turn away when others need help, who selflessly gives to others and puts themselves last. One who strives to do good even when others put obstacles in their way and never gives up, even when everything seems meaningless. The heart sees and understands everything; we just need to listen to it. ⋮ Not everything is what it seems at first glance. Spontaneity can be very helpful at times, and taking time to think about what you've seen, heard, and read. Sometimes a simple drawing or word holds much more meaning than it appears at first glance. Maybe there isn't any deeper meaning, but it still helps to listen to the author, try to understand them, and ask questions to make it easier to understand. The saying still holds true that the wise ask questions. Without asking, you may not discover the essence hidden in a hat. This hat reminds me of many other things, besides what the Little Prince represented. We must let our imagination be surprised. Believe me, you'll be positively surprised by the breadth of thoughts your mind can bring you. ⋮ It's always worth waiting

for better times. After all, everything in life is just a brief moment. Nothing lasts forever. Every situation has a beginning and an end. If something's not going well, hold on because better times are just around the corner. And if things are going well, cherish every moment and make the most of it. Life is unpredictable, but that's what makes it so

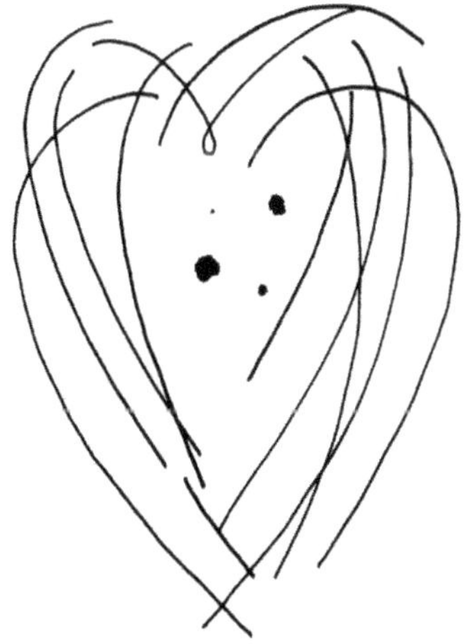

exciting. Embrace the unknown and enjoy the journey. ⁝ The Little Prince represents one character that teaches us how life works and shows us the direction to improve it. All we have to do is let him guide us in his own unique way. Each of us can be our own Little Prince, revealing our experiences, insights, and thoughts to others and leading them toward a better life. Without Little Princes, we wouldn't survive. Be your own Little Prince, using your wisdom to explore the mysteries of your own planet and the depths of humanity. ⁝ I add that wisdom can be gained with age, but it's not necessarily a given. ⁞

Personal growth occurs gradually. It's hard to pinpoint a breakthrough moment. Every day, it was a breakthrough when I did something differently and responded more wisely to what happened to me. But one thing had a more profound impact on me before and after, and that's meditation. Meditation helps us transcend the influence of our analytical mind and delve into the subconscious. That's also its main purpose. In the subconscious lie all of our bad habits and behavioral patterns that we want to change. Meditation helps us change our behavior, emotional responses, self-destructive habits, beliefs, and attitudes. It helps us redirect our attention from our environment, body, and time to our intentions and thoughts. In short, it helps us transform from who we are into who we want to become.

Being grateful for the good things in life is easy. All we need to do is remember not to take them for granted and express our gratitude. The real challenge is being thankful for the unpleasant and harmful things that happen to us. ⦂ At times, it can feel like everything is conspiring against us. That's what I thought on a particular day when it seemed like all the forces were against me. First, I couldn't leave the public garage because the gate wouldn't lift. When I finally managed to escape, I hit another roadblock with a part of the city being closed for a bike race. It took me quite some time to navigate my way out of the center of Ljubljana through various detours. ⦂ I encountered a traffic accident just before my destination that I would have probably been involved in without the earlier obstacles. That's when I learned to be grateful for life's unpleasant and harmful things. In this case, they aimed to prevent me from getting into a traffic accident. ⦂ Then, I thought someone or something was guiding and looking after me. ⦂ Now I know that life always provides me with the best experience. I no longer resist what happens. I no longer see things as good or bad. I am completely relaxed and unafraid. ⦂ I've stopped worrying about things I can't control, stopped taking things too seriously, and surrendered (with room for improvement). The joy is immense. ⦂ As an ancient sage once said, »The path is smooth. Why do you keep putting rocks in your way?« ⦂⦂

I knew that humans have a soul, but I never imagined that we could communicate with it. When I delved into Nikola Tesla's works, I learned of this possibility. Tesla, the man who invented the future, wasn't just an exceptional scientist, but a deeply spiritual human being who gifted the world with alternating current, the radio, wireless transmission of energy and communication, remote control, robotics, lighting, and the AC induction motor. ⁝ I was introduced to Klemen, a true master of communicating with souls. It was a challenge that I took on out of sheer curiosity. I wanted to know what my soul had to say. The conversation was in complete silence while I sat beside him, engrossed in a book. It lasted half an hour, and I must admit that I was a bit nervous. Klemen took notes of everything my soul revealed to him and handed them to me after the session. ⁝

The Conversation Between Klemen and My Soul: ⁝ »Marjana, hello. How can I help you today?« ⁝ »Well, see, I don't know. I like that I can delve deeper into my knowledge and understanding of myself, which excites me. I've been aware for a long time of how different my boundaries and limits are and how far I can go. It's incredible. My inner insights are so strong, genuine, and intense that it all becomes infinitely interesting. It's like a big stage where I'm finally the lead actor. I've often been used in life as an exceptional 'support.' It sounds funny, but I've acted 'behind the scenes' for quite some time. ⁝ »It took me a while to allow myself to take on the lead actor role in my life.

And you know what I'm going to say? I'm enjoying it. A lot. To the point where I want to scream. And it feels good. And I don't want to cross myself for anyone anymore. No. Enough is enough. I've often tried to force my way out—as something happy. But the effect was never within my expectations. Yes, now it is. ⠿ »Don't think that I talk about myself because I'm bragging. Not at all. I just love living my life. That's with a capital *L*. I've always wanted to express this to you, not because you wouldn't understand it, but because these are significant discoveries for me. I've always loved living; it's never been a question. It could be because I knew how to find happiness in small things. But in my mind, I've always wanted to reach for the stars. My inner world of imagination was incredibly rich. I'm aware of that. But I didn't share it often. I wanted it to be mine, completely mine. I don't talk much about myself in general. I always act the same—I give a clue or direction, if you will, where the conversation or energy is headed, and then I just relax and think. ⠿ »I'm so good at evaluating situations that it can get boring sometimes. When I think about it, it might be true that I can look into the future. Clairvoyance? Maybe. New things are coming for me that will deepen my knowledge and understanding of the world, myself, and relationships. As a good observer, I've always loved observing relationships. Not just between people. Relationships in general. Who or what is in a relationship with whom or what … and that always fed my curious soul. So much can be seen, even if you don't look. And my specialty—reading between the lines. I wonder if that falls under the category of the sixth sense. I experience my 'reading' multi-dimensionally. Different from what's expected. The conclusions and findings are inspiring. I don't know how to describe this skill of mine. If I describe it with 'x-ray,' it sounds too technical; 'reading,' too predictable; 'sensing,' without any sense—it would take away my credibility, for God's sake. I'm a woman who wants a good reputation. So I always know how, and maintaining my dignity has always been possible. I like that, but lately I've noticed that I have too much energy because of it. ⋮ »It's becoming more challenging for me to solve problems in a friendly way when I'm bored or not being fed enough by my inner child. And you know what's happening to me? I physically start to sway. ⋮ »Maybe it's time for me to let go of my tight grip on 'what is right' and allow myself to go wild. I tend to control myself too much and become bored in situations that are 'under control.' I am trying to understand why this happens. A restlessness whispers to me, telling me to let go. But how can I let go when I'm so well-equipped for leadership? That would actually be quite the challenge for me—to release control. To let go, yes. To surrender, no. No, no, and no. That's not good for me. Or is it?« ⋮ »I don't know. Tell me, what do you feel when you hear 'surrender?' What does it evoke in you?« ⋮ »For me, it evokes a youthful excitement. An inner laugh. It calls to me, like sirens calling to a sailor. It ignites something new within me, something I don't really know.

I'm still weak when it comes to surrendering. But it's getting better. This may be something new. For me to be unrestrained, with all the power I have within me. The thought alone is sinful. But it excites me. And brings sparks to my eyes. So there's something special about this challenge. Would I'd be good at it? I have no problems with planning, but I wouldn't say the same for being spontaneous. I need experience. So much is yet to come. I like it—like turbulent water. I've always jumped into the clear, sparkling water. But now, the mist is calling to me. When I should break away from the ground and fly into the unknown, my 'unknown' was always discovered within the limits of what I could see. But what's happening now is a journey into absolute mystery. ⋮ »See, Klemen, this is all moving in the direction I wanted. What my soul wants from me, I'll have to accept. Face the unknown beyond the limits of the known. I like it, and I have no shortage of courage. I want to face myself. It's good for me and those around me. No matter how big the challenge, I've said yes to myself. I feel good. My inner world is changing. Challenges are coming. I feel good. I'm happy to be who I am. And so, I'll allow myself to try »over there,« but I don't want to talk about it anymore. Thank you.« ⋮ It was a weight off my shoulders when Klemen read this conversation. That's how it is. I have many challenges ahead of me. ⋮ I'm looking forward to them. ⋮ Talking to my soul through Klemen was a profound experience. I felt empowered and connected to something greater than myself. Now, I can access this part of myself whenever I need guidance or insight. As Tesla once said, »My brain is only a receiver, in the Universe there is a core from which we obtain knowledge, strength, and inspiration. I have not penetrated into the secrets of this core, but I know that it exists.« ⋮ With this newfound knowledge, I feel confident and productive, ready to take on whatever life throws my way. ⦂

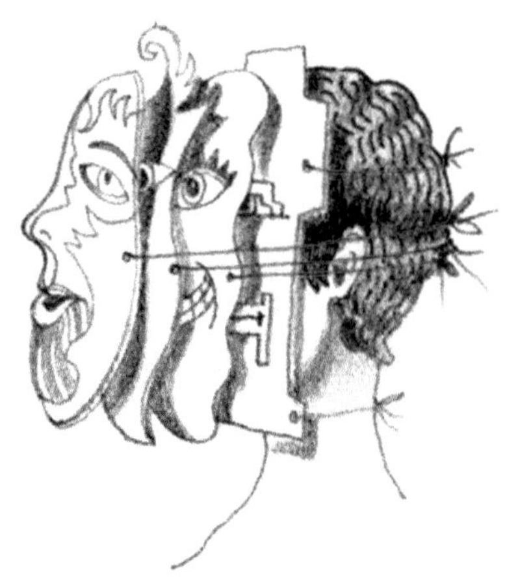

Why do we wear shields? Out of fear. We feel vulnerable and fear abandonment. We lack confidence and courage. We don't trust. We don't understand. We don't trust that all departures and losses have a purpose and that everything will be as it should be. ⋮ We must stop clinging to what is departing and learn to let go. Everything that has fulfilled its purpose will eventually disappear. We need to embrace the plan that we may not yet understand. At some point, we will realize that it's easier to accept change than to fight it. ⋮ Changing the way we see ourselves may be the toughest challenge we'll face in our lives. When we realize that life brings us exactly what we need, when we need it, and that we are always prepared for everything life throws our way, fear disappears. That's when we're ready to put down our shields. ⋮ Only then do we realize the weight we've been carrying and how our shield was hindering our movement. Only then do we recognize that our shield wasn't protecting us but limiting us. Only then, when we put it down, do we take a deep breath and run confidently toward new adventures, knowing everything will be okay. Because we know that everything that happens has its own purpose and meaning. ⋮ The shield begins to melt when emotions surface, when there's no longer a need to justify ourselves or our transgressors, and when we allow ourselves to be vulnerable again to make mistakes. ⁚⁚

Since I started writing a journal, my life has improved. Every day, I try to experience or do something worth writing about. It's worth noting the things that have taught us something, given us something, touched us, and left their mark on us. Writing brings a certain kind of relief. It allows us to be completely open and, at the same time, organize our thoughts. ⋮

From my journal: ⋮ For the past few years, I've felt like I was undergoing a transformation. It was most like the development of a caterpillar into a butterfly. ⋮ From the egg, the caterpillar emerges, and then it cocoons itself, focusing again on a point where it has put all its physical body before. The caterpillar dies, but the cocoon protects it from external forces to create a new life with a new quality. From the cocoon, the butterfly emerges. ⋮ At first, I felt like a caterpillar—cute, tiny, and green, a caterpillar that had to

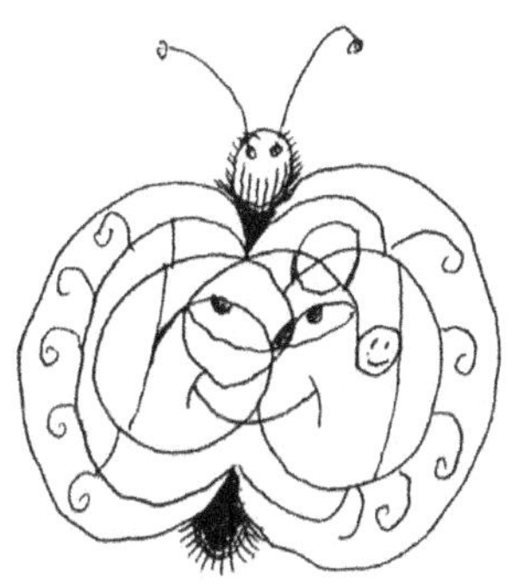

change its skin every so often because it became too small. Then, like a caterpillar, I anchored my head down and started spinning silky threads. I wrapped and wrapped and created a beautiful, warm, and safe cocoon. I became a cocoon. After a while, the cocoon became solid armor. I felt very safe inside it. I thought this was my transformation's final stage and that I would live safely and comfortably in this solid armor. ⋮ But it happened that I continued to develop. So there needed to be more space and air in the armor. At one point, the cocoon started

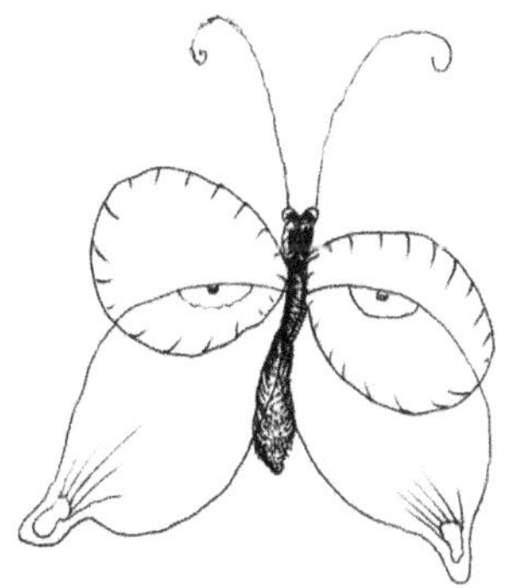

to open. A woman peeked out. At first, she was a bit uncertain and confused, but then she became more beautiful, stronger, and radiant day by day. ⫶ The transformation was complete. The caterpillar had developed into a brave, mature, and wise woman who, like a butterfly, spread her wings and flew toward new adventures. Free. ⫶ The essence of life in this process is that a living organism arises from growth. Then the life force in this organism discards its body, withdraws, gathers, transforms, and then releases into shaping new life quality—in the invisible realm that leaves traces in the visible. ⁞

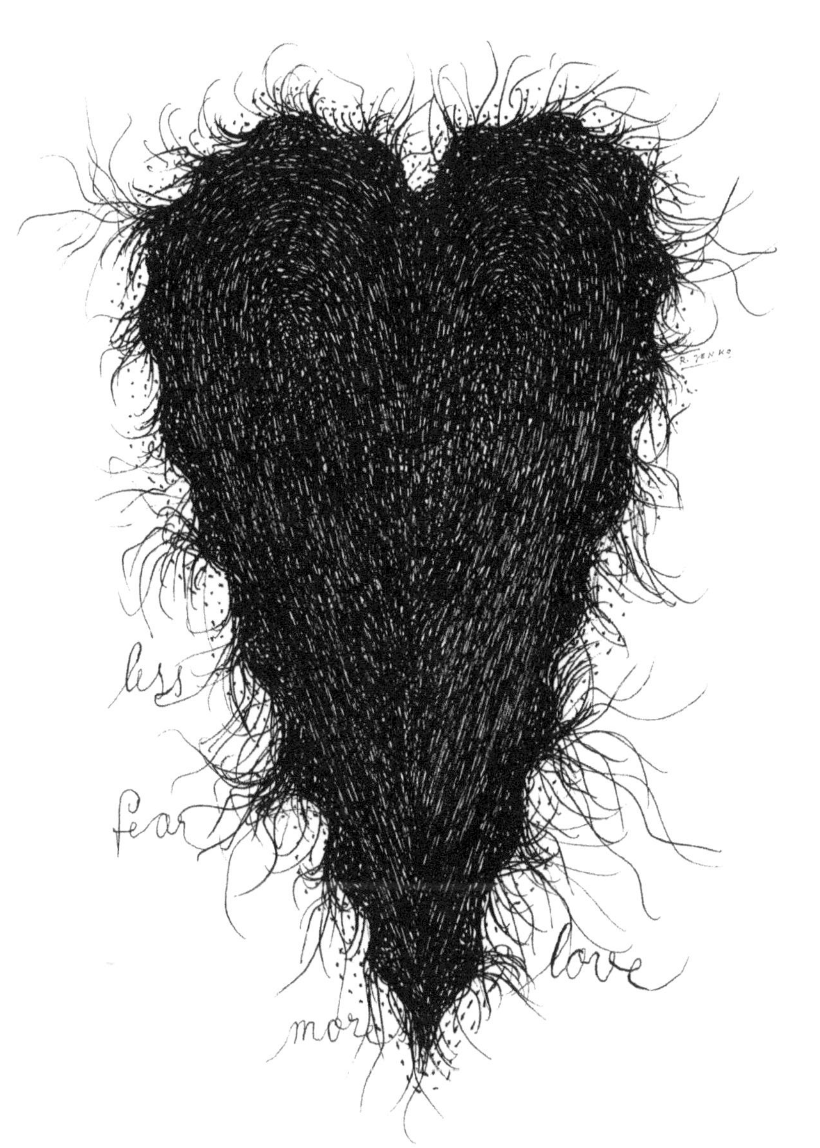

less
fear
more
love

At the writing of the last chapter of this book, the Covid-19 pandemic had begun. What has the epidemic taught us, and what should we not forget until the next such experience?

> The things we devote most of our time to may not be so important after all,

> there's no need to be available every moment,

> taking time to reflect is not just necessary; it's essential,

> the time we spend on ourselves and our loved ones is valuable,

> it's time to re-evaluate our priorities,

> we should be creative,

> we should be rational,

> we should be compassionate,

> treating nature with kindness will lead to greater abundance in return,

> and it's time to finally finish the things we've been putting off for so long . . .

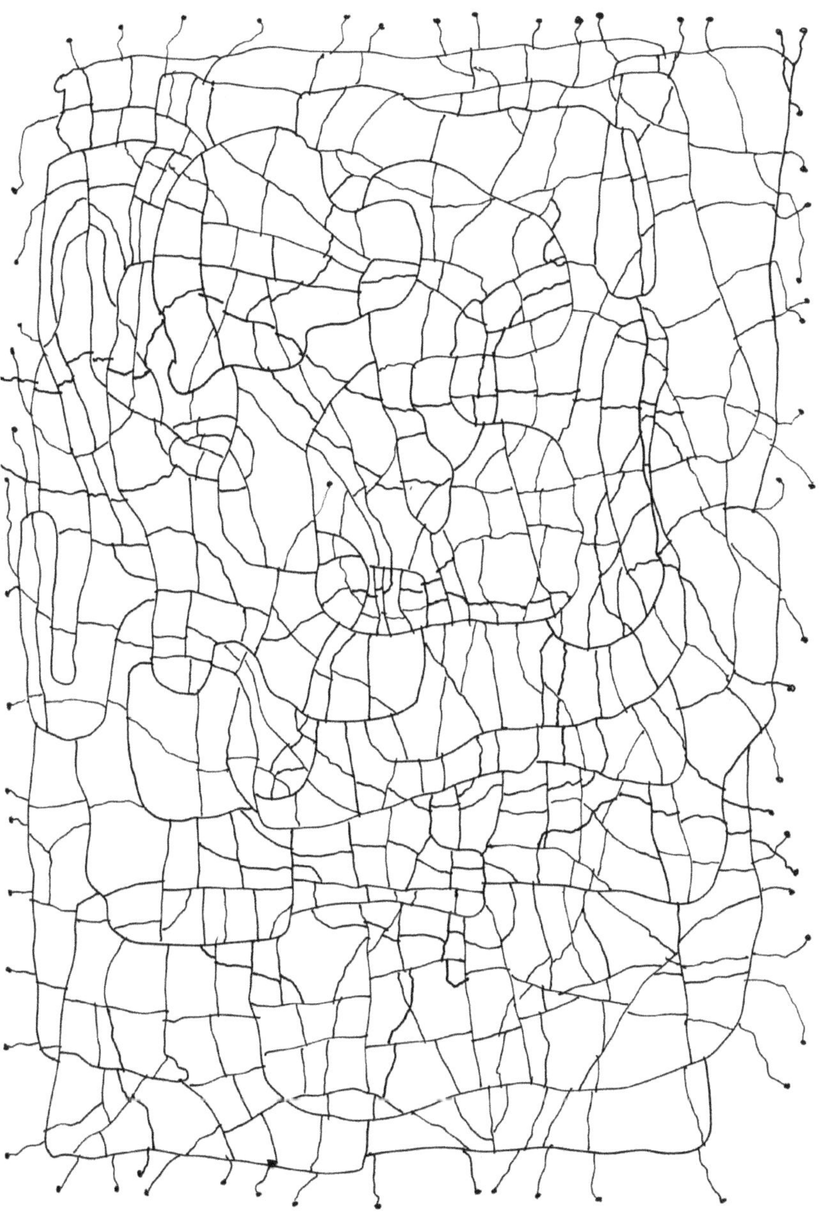

When we realize that everything is exactly as it should be, life becomes easier, and we can move from resistance to flow. Being in the flow means trusting, allowing, and accepting even what our minds cannot comprehend. It means letting go of control. Flow is an energy that flows, and nothing can stop it. Let it flow. Flow relaxes you, makes life easier, and enriches it. Flow helps you live. You just have to dare. Being in the flow means not interfering with the creations that life brings us with our limited minds. When we are in the flow, we realize that our lives can be much more beautiful than when we try to force them to fit our limited vision. Flow makes life smoother and richer while we smile at how everything falls into place precisely as it should. ⦙ When you let go of resistance and enter the flow, life becomes incredibly light, and you never want to return to the way things were. Finally, you start enjoying life. Trust yourself, trust the flow, and trust that everything happens for a reason at the right time. You can achieve anything and live the desired life when you are in the flow. ⁝⁝

The path to finding oneself is unique and can be complicated. It's made up of decisions. Even »wrong« decisions are correct, although we don't see them as such now. The decisions we make determine the length and direction of our journey. ⋮ The path can be difficult at the beginning of the journey, and we may stumble, fall, and get scraped. But as we keep walking, we gain more experience, and the path becomes friendlier. The rocks under our feet become smoother and easier to navigate. We can see further and find it easier to orient ourselves. ⋮ Throughout the journey, people accompany us. Some push us deeper, while others lift us up. Everyone comes at the right time and stays with us for as long as necessary, but not a minute longer. Once we realize this, we can easily thank even those who hurt us on this journey. ⋮ When we finally find ourselves, we feel lighter, free from all the burdens we've knowingly or unknowingly carried, and we push off and fly. We truly start living.

I finally feel like I've arrived at the highway, after years of driving on dirt roads, bumpy and rough paths, and blind alleys. What a relief. Now I can step on the gas and continue my journey on the smooth and fast road. Of course, this doesn't mean I won't miss an exit or get a speeding ticket occasionally. But these will be just »little mistakes« that will excite my journey and teach me something new as I venture into the unknown. ⋮ The richness of life can only be felt by letting go of fear and embracing the unknown. Nothing starts if something doesn't end. Establishing a new relationship with the unknown is critical to embarking on a new beginning. ⋮ *»In search of peace, I've spent most of my life trying to either relive the past or predict the future, until I finally realized that peace lies precisely in the middle of these two extremes.«*

Unknown author ⁞

Dear Iza and Živa, ⁝ You may have realized I didn't share anything new with you as you read through these pages. Perhaps, this realization left you feeling frustrated. ⁝ Or, perhaps, you realized that even though you already knew everything I shared, you still haven't taken any action, causing you to feel angry with yourselves. ⁝ Maybe you realized that I didn't share anything new, but the reminder of past promises you made to yourselves was a welcome one. ⁝ And maybe, I shared something new with you after all. ⁝ Regardless of what you took away from this, I'm glad you're a part of my life, and I hope we'll experience many more beautiful moments together. ⁝ I love you both. *Marjana* ⁞

I thank everyone who entered my life and helped me become who I am today. Without all of you, I wouldn't have succeeded, even without those who appeared in my life for a very short time. This also counts; this also leaves a trace. Thank you, therefore, to all those who have known me and already forgotten me, to those who know me and are still part of my life, and thank you also to those who will only enter my life in the future. Time is a relative thing. With the help of all of you, this book was created. Thank you.

Marjana Robavs worked for many years as a media director at one of Slovenia's largest and most creative advertising agencies—Futura DDB. There, she gained a deep understanding of people's habits, needs, and behaviors. ⁝ However, Marjana's passion for her work had faded, and she knew it was time for a change. ⁝ She believes that exceptional results can only be achieved when one works with passion and enjoyment, which she has gladly found in her new work. ⁝ The inspiration for this book is the knowledge and experience she has gained from her own life. She firmly believes that everything happens for a reason and every life situation is a lesson from which we can learn and grow. ⁝ This unique approach to life has led to numerous insights and discoveries that she shares with her readers. ⁝⁝

THOUGHTS

Published by:
ROBAVS MARJANA s. p. – KLICK
Brdnikova ulica 60, SI-1000 Ljubljana, Slovenia
https://marjanarobavs.com/
Email: marjana.robavs@gmail.com

Illustrations and Design:
RADOVAN JENKO

First Edition 2023

Print on demand

Kataložni zapis o publikaciji (CIP)
pripravili v Narodni in univerzitetni knjižnici v Ljubljani
130.2(035)
ROBAVS, Marjana
The art of living and learning : a guide to unlocking your inner strenght and potencial /
Marjana Robavs ; illustrations Radovan Jenko.- 1st ed. - Ljubljana : Klick, 2023
COBISS.SI-ID 161188611
ISBN 978-961-07-1708-9 (ePUB)
ISBN 978-961-07-1703-4 (hc)
ISBN 978-961-07-1697-6 (pbk)

www.ingramcontent.com/pod-product-compliance
Lightning Source LLC
Chambersburg PA
CBHW041203150726
48006CB00016B/2088